RESOURCES, TARIFFS, AND TRADE:
ONTARIO'S STAKE

J. R. Williams

Resources, Tariffs, and Trade: Ontario's stake

PUBLISHED FOR THE ONTARIO ECONOMIC COUNCIL BY
UNIVERSITY OF TORONTO PRESS
TORONTO AND BUFFALO

Library of Congress Cataloging in Publication Data

Williams, James Richard Mackenzie, 1923-
  Resources, tariffs, and trade.

(Ontario Economic Council Research studies; 6)
1. Ontario — Commerce. 2. Tariff — Canada. 3. Commercial products —
Canada. 4. Ontario — Economic conditions. I. Title. II. Series: Ontario
Economic Council. Ontario Economic Council research studies; 6.
HF3229.05W54   382.7'09713   76-26043
ISBN 0-8020-3340-7 pbk.

This study reflects the views of the author and not necessarily those of the
Ontario Economic Council.

Contents

Preface

From the point of view of the individual firm or its employees, tariffs appear to provide a necessary level of protection against foreign competition and hence to confer only benefits, with no adverse effects. Only occasionally after becoming aware of the difference between the cost of some consumer item in Canada and its cost abroad is one induced to consider the possible adverse effects of tariffs. In fact, the protective effects of the tariff are much more visible and appear stronger to the casual observer than they really are. The adverse effects of the tariff are, by comparison, more subtle and do not become apparent except through comprehensive study. This is why one finds that the general public is usually more favourably disposed toward tariff protection than is the professional economist.

In this monograph I have tried to present the ideas of one professional economist. As explained in the introduction to chapter 1, tariff protection in any industry must have repercussions on all industries. A tariff may protect some enterprises competing with imports, thus encouraging a higher level of output, but typically this is achieved with a loss of production and employment in firms belonging to the export sector. In addition, the tariff adds to the costs of consumer goods. In designing its tariff, Canada is aiding some industries to expand while forcing others to contract. Which industries should be favoured and which should not?

It is the working hypothesis adopted in this study that Canada should specialize in those areas of production where, given her endowment of capital, labour, and resources, she is best able to compete internationally. In the first chapter, the underlying theory relating to this hypothesis is reviewed. It is a matter of common belief, corroborated by the empirical evidence of chapter 2 and by an excellent study recently released by the Economic Council of Canada (Postner, 1975), that Canada can best compete at later stages of processing by producing goods which utilize those resources most abundant in Canada as compared to the rest of the world. In chapter 2 the reader will find a detailed review of the resource basis of Canada's comparative advantage. Also, evidence is presented (based on another study forthcoming) to the effect that, under free trade, Canada's productive base would shift toward the end stage of processing.

Chapter 3 examines the relationship between resource use, processing, and tariffs in Canada, the United States, the EEC, and Japan to determine the likely effect of these tariffs on trade. The final chapter is an attempt to relate these matters to the situation in Ontario. The most general conclusion from the evidence is that the Canadian tariff does not support the growth of Ontario manufacturing relative to other provinces, although it probably has had the effect of encouraging relatively greater agricultural production in Ontario than would be the case in free trade. Ontario's best prospects seem to lie in the processing of minerals and metals other than iron ore. Protection of the iron and steel sector seems to have had the greatest adverse effect in Ontario outside the iron and steel sector itself. This is because the iron and steel sector is an important supplier to other industries, and the tariff therefore increases the cost of intermediate goods in Canada in user industries, reducing the competitiveness of Canadian industries outside the iron and steel sector.

In so far as this study may prove helpful in assessing the effect of Canada's tariff in Ontario, it is due to the aid of many people, including the chairman of the Ontario Economic Council, Dr Grant Reuber, who suggested the initial line of research. I have also benefited from many conversations with my friends in the Ontario government from whom I have gained a better understanding of the policy issues involved. I would particularly like to mention Mr David Redgrave, executive director, Office of Economic Policy, Mr Brock Smith, director, Policy Planning Branch, and Mr John Elliot, now director, Regional Analysis, Government of British Columbia. Also I am most grateful for the cooperation of Mr Brian Salley, assistant director, External Trade Division in Ottawa, and Mr Rob Hoffman, director, Structural Analysis Division, who supplied data and technical advice. Finally, I must mention the conscientious assistance of Mrs Margaret Derrah who helped with the computations. Of course, none of the above are responsible for (nor would they necessarily agree with) my conclusions and they should not be held responsible for any errors or omissions in the manuscript.

RESOURCES, TARIFFS, AND TRADE:
ONTARIO'S STAKE

1
Conceptual aspects of this study

INTRODUCTION

The industrial impact of Canada's tariff is an exceedingly complex matter involving much more than could be covered in any single project. This study is an inquiry into the relationship between Canada's tariff schedule, and her comparative advantage, in so far as this latter is influenced by the Canadian resource base.

For the purpose of such a study two fundamental identities are of considerable importance. The first of these is the balance-of-payments identity. The amount of foreign exchange earned from exports or borrowed from abroad must equal exactly the amount of foreign exchange used to purchase imports or lent abroad. The effect of this identity can be illustrated if we consider the impact of an increased tariff on employment. Let us assume for the moment that the tariff has no effect on net foreign lending and that it succeeds in reducing imports of commodities competitive with Canadian production. Because of the balance-of-payments identity we know that under the assumed circumstances there must be a reduction of equal value in Canadian exports. Unless there is a change in foreign lending, the tariff will not succeed as an instrument for increasing the level of productive activity in Canada, and it may either increase or decrease employment.

The tariff will increase employment if each dollar of increased production in the import-competing sector requires more labour than an equivalent dollar reduction in the export sector. It is true for employment and for any non-economic argument in favour of tariffs that an implicit comparison is involved between industries which compete with imports (and which, therefore, expand under protection) and industries which are export-oriented (and which, therefore, contract as foreign sales decline under the tariff). If, contrary to assumption, the tariff should induce an increase in net foreign investment in Canada, this proposition needs to be modified. It is clear from the balance-of-payments identity that in this case the reduction in exports must *exceed* the reduction in imports. The balance-of-payments identity demonstrates that the tariff cannot reduce imports more than it reduces exports, except in the case where there is an increase in net Canadian investment in foreign nations.

The second accounting identity relates to the value of processed commodities and the cost of the resources needed to produce processed commodities. The value of commodity exports must be exactly equal to the cost of resources (land, labour, and capital) required to produce exports.[1] Therefore, all trade can be resolved into an equivalent in resource trade. Some resources are exported directly without further processing while others are sold as part of the cost of exported commodities. The sum of these two must equal the value of total exports. Similarly, the value of resources imported directly without further processing plus imports as part of the cost of commodities must also equal the total value of imports. If the tariff does not affect private decisions to lend or borrow from abroad, every dollar increase (or decrease) in imports is matched by an equal increase (or decrease) in exports, and any change in the value of resources exported must be equal to the change in the value of resources imported.

On the basis of the last identity we can establish a useful result. The more trade flows through processed commodities, the more it must become a reflection of resources. Indeed, if there is no direct trade in resources at all, the exchange of resources must be conducted entirely through commodities. Canada's exports of labour, for example, are equivalent to the cost of the labour required to produce commodity exports. It is a truism in economics that the greatest gains are derived when one exchanges that which is in abundance for that which is scarce. If resources are completely immobile between nations and if Canada follows the logic of exchanging her abundant resources based on agriculture and mining for scarce labour, this would have to be reflected in commodity trade, with imported commodities being produced relatively more from labour and exported commodities being produced relatively more from the resources of land.

---

1 This follows from the fact that the income earned in each firm must be equal to its sales less the cost of intermediate goods and that such income must be paid to one of the factors of production.

This point is the underlying theme of this study, but it is not intended to suggest that such consideration is the sole or overriding concern of commercial policy. Convincing evidence suggests, for example, that Canada would gain from the increased competition of free trade and that the associated elimination of foreign tariffs would bring further gains through economies of scale as Canadian producers would then be able to penetrate the larger markets of the United States and the EEC (Wonnacott and Wonnacott, 1967; Eastman and Stykolt, 1967). It is assumed in this study that free trade is not among the options open to Canada. We are concerned, rather, with the type of tariff change that one would expect from the GATT negotiations currently in session. It is intended in this research to provide some helpful guidance to those interested in obtaining a better understanding of the options open to Canada and Ontario under these circumstances.

THE HECKSCHER-OHLIN THEOREM

The specialist in international economics will have already recognized that this study is greatly influenced by what is known in the literature as the Heckscher-Ohlin, or Factor Proportions, Theorem.[2] According to this theorem, differences in the proportions in which resources are distributed internationally are an important factor determining trade in processed commodities. A country will export those commodities which are produced from the nation's abundant resources and import processed commodities which are produced from the nation's scarce resources.

The intuitive basis for the theorem is rather easily explained. In the absence of trade the cost of the various resources (including labour) would differ between nations. Wages should be lowest in the nations where labour is most abundant relative to, say, land, and highest where labour is scarce relative to land. On the other hand, land rent would be lower in nations where it is abundant relative to labour and higher in nations where it is scarce. Commodities which require a large amount of labour relative to land would be cheaper in the labour-abundant nations and the commodities requiring a relatively large amount of land in production would be cheaper in the nations abundant in land. With trade, the cheaper labour-intensive exports of the labour-abundant nation would be exchanged for the cheaper land-intensive exports of the land-abundant

---

2 The theorem first appears in the writings of Eli Heckscher. The key article was written in Swedish, but is available in English translation as 'The effect of foreign trade on the distribution of income,' in Ellis and Metzler (1950). Later the idea was extensively developed by Ohlin (1933, rev. 1967).

nation. In the thought of Heckscher there were two prerequisites for trade. There must be differences in resource abundance among nations, and the resource proportions required to produce one commodity must differ from the resource proportions required to produce others.

It was implicit in the Heckscher-Ohlin Theorem that the prices of resources, although different in autarky, would begin to equalize with trade. The costs of the commodities requiring relatively more labour to produce would be lower in the labour-abundant nations than in other nations, and hence exports and production of labour-intensive commodities would expand. This would increase the demand for labour in the labour-abundant nation and thereby increase the wage of labour. In the land-abundant nation where, prior to trade, the rents would be relatively low, there would be an increase in demand for land-intensive commodities, raising rents in the land-abundant nation. The theorem seemed to carry with it, therefore, the implication that the prices of resources would tend toward equality and perhaps be completely equalized through trade. If so, it would be one of the consequences of trade that differences in comparative advantage would disappear. The theoretical aspects of this question have a literature which is too extensive to review in this study (Stolper and Samuelson, 1941-2; Samuelson, 1953-4). It should be stated, however, that the assumptions usually employed to obtain a mathematical proof of the Factor Proportions Theorem are also sufficient to prove mathematically that resource prices are equalized among nations.[3] In this model of the Factor Proportions Theorem, therefore, the cost of similar industries located in different nations appear to be exactly the same in the observed equilibrium, but the slopes of their respective long-run cost schedules would differ in a manner first described by Robinson (1941. For a more modern treatment see Rybczynski, 1955). If any particular industry should expand beyond the level observed in equilibrium, it would raise the unit cost of the resources required in greatest proportion by the expanding industry; hence, in the process of expanding the expanding firm would raise its own average cost above the costs of similar industries located abroad. In the absence of economies of scale, long-run costs would rise as output expanded but the rate of increase would be different in different nations depending on relative resource supplies.

The mathematical model of the Factor Proportions Theorem stated in connection with factor-price equalization is highly abstract, and the assumptions required are very unrealistic. However, it is clear from the literature and from intuition that factor-price equalization is not a condition necessary as far as the

---

3   See Vanek (1968) for a list of the assumptions sufficient for the Theorem

Heckscher-Ohlin Theorem is concerned.[4] It is assumed in the mathematical proof, for example, that there are no tariffs and that transport costs are zero, but these are in fact forces which prevent trade and thereby maintain the cost of commodities lower at the point where resources are in greater supply. Despite its abstract nature, the mathematical version of the Factor Proportions Theorem has aided research by pointing to statistical constructs which are needed in empirical studies. It also indicates an alternative avenue to intuitive understanding of the theorem.

Following Baldwin (1971) one may explain the theorem in terms of resource consumption and resource supplies. If we have a world correctly described by the factor-price equalization theorem with identical tastes in all nations, the factor proportions used to produce each commodity would be the same in each nation and hence consumption of resources would be proportionally the same in each. Only through trade would it be possible for nations differing in the proportions in which resources are supplied to be exactly identical in the proportions in which resources are used. Each nation would import commodities produced from resources in short supply and export commodities produced from abundant resources.

The use of resources in production of commodities is, of course, a key point in this type of analysis. The reader will need to distinguish between the direct use of resources and the indirect use of resources. This distinction was first clarified in the literature of international economics by Leontief (1954; 1956). Direct resource use refers to the amount actually purchased by the firm or establishment responsible for the processing. Indirect resource use refers to the additional amount of resources required to produce all of the intermediate commodities required in production. The food processing industry, for example, may make no direct purchases of wheat, but wheat is required to make bread. The wheat is obtained as part of the cost of flour. Flour is the intermediate product. If every firm produced all of its required intermediate goods, the intermediate product purchases would vanish and in each firm the *production* of intermediate commodities would be equal to what in practice we observe as direct plus indirect *purchases* of intermediate goods. Also, the direct purchases of resources of such a firm would be equal to all of the resources which are now purchased directly and indirectly. The reader is referred to the mathematical appendix for further technical explanation.

4 The theorem is appraised, under the assumption that factor prices are not equalized, in Bertrand (1972). Also see Bardhan (1965), in which conditions relating to production functions are relaxed. Another example can be found in Bhagwati (1972). Bhagwati has shown that an important extension of the Factor Proportions Theorem due to Jones will not hold unless the required assumptions are made more realistic by introducing transport costs. See Jones (1956-7).

CRITICISMS OF THE HECKSCHER-OHLIN THEOREM

There is now an extensive literature on the empirical aspects of the Heckscher-Ohlin Theorem. Part of it is intended to test the applicability[5] of the theorem with regard to a particular nation and part is intended to extend the original Leontief conceptual framework (noted above) by adding variables to account for factors which, in a narrow interpretation, would be omitted. Hufbauer (1970, 147) lists the following seven explanations for trade:

1 Nations export commodities which require relatively large amounts of abundant resources. This is the Factor Proportions Theorem in its strict form.

2 The relative abundance of professional personnel and highly trained labour promotes exports from some nations while relative abundance of unskilled labour promotes exports from others. This can be regarded as an elaboration of the Factor Proportions Theorem.

3 Because of large home markets, some nations export goods produced under increasing returns to scale and import goods produced under constant returns to scale.[6]

4 Some nations may be specialized in sophisticated producer goods and others in light consumer goods.

5 Early manufacture of new goods confers an export advantage, while producers in other nations must rely on lower wages and other static features.

6 Sophistication and early manufacture leads to export of differentiated consumer goods, while lack of sophistication leads to export of standard goods.

7 Similarity of tastes in two nations leads to intensive trade between them.

This is by no means an exclusive list,[7] and many other theories will likely be needed to explain the thousands of commodity trade flows between nations. It should be noted, however, that none of the above is inconsistent with the Heckscher-Ohlin Theorem, which in its broadest sense merely asserts that resource abundance is an important source of comparative advantage in the production of certain commodities. In so far as comparative costs may have

---

5 Unfortunately the tests of the theorem have been inconclusive. In Leontief's original work, cited above, the data did not seem to support the hypothesis that the Heckscher-Ohlin Theorem was valid in the case of the United States. It has been argued since, however, that these data should be interpreted as supporting the theorem (see Williams, 1970, 121). Using later data and regression methods, Baldwin (1971) also found that the theorem was contradicted by United States data. These data were later analysed by Harkness and Kyle, however, who found that they did, in fact, support the Heckscher-Ohlin Theorem (see Harkness and Kyle, 1975).

6 An interesting discussion of this point can be found in Melvin (1969).

7 For example, tariffs are omitted from the list. Travis (1964; 1972) has argued that these are very important as a determinant of commodity trade.

some degree of priority in tariff policy considerations, the reader will find the results outlined below of interest.

Another line of criticism is directed at the logical foundations of the Heckscher-Ohlin Theorem. Here also is a rather extensive literature,[8] so that our comments are confined to those criticisms brought out in connection with empirical studies of American data (which have been more extensively analysed than those of any other nation). Baldwin (1971) notes six major criticisms. Three represent alternative explanations for trade and are covered by Hufbauer's list above (if we add tariffs). In addition, Baldwin notes three criticisms directed at the logical foundations of the theorem.

1 As noted, Heckscher regarded it as one of the prerequisites of the Factor Proportions Theorem that the proportions in which resources are required in the production of any commodity must differ from every other. In order for the theorem to be useful, a ranking of commodities according to their proportional use of resources cannot change when factor prices change. If the ratio of land to labour used in commodity 1, for example, is greater than the same ratio for commodity 2 for some given wage and rental, it must be true for all relevant values of wages and rentals. If this is not true we would have what is known in the literature as factor-intensity reversals. Under such circumstances it is no longer possible to determine in advance which commodities make the greatest use of the abundant resources, nor is it possible to say which commodities will be exported. Earlier research seemed to indicate that factor reversals were quite probable, but subsequent analysis has indicated the opposite.[9]

2 It was above asserted that the Heckscher-Ohlin Theorem regarded from one perspective is merely a rigorous way of stating the conditions under which it would be logically inevitable that each nation would consume resources in exactly the same proportion as every other. If we then assume, as in Baldwin's illustration, that resources are supplied in different proportions in each nation, trade then serves the function of reallocating resources. Abundant resources are given up through exported commodities, and scarce resources are acquired through imported commodities. One criticism of the Heckscher-Ohlin Theorem holds that resource consumption is far from proportional, some nations' tastes may depart so much from the rest of the world that resources abundant by world standards are consumed internally or imported, while those which are scarce by world standards are little used and perhaps exported. Although this

---

8 An older but still frequently quoted critique is Robinson (1956). For a more recent critique see Michaely (1964).
9 See Leontief (1964), Yahr (1968), Philpot (1970), and Ball (1970). The earlier position critical of the Heckscher-Ohlin Theorem is developed in Minhas (1963).

criticism is acknowledged as a theoretical possibility, no writer has as yet argued that this departure from the theorem constitutes a substantial exception.

3 In connection with US data, it has been argued that the complementarity between capital and resources is so great that the United States would need to import 'abundant capital' as part of the value of 'scarce' resources imported and hence would be a net importer of both. Baldwin (1971, 129) has shown that this argument is illogical: 'In the case where natural resource industries are capital-intensive and natural resources are scarce in a capital-abundant country, factor equilibrium may be achieved in two ways: By the capital-abundant country exporting items that are even more capital using than natural resource products; or by the rest of the world, which is labour abundant, exporting highly labour-intensive commodities in addition to the capital intensive, natural resource products.'

DEFINITION OF RESOURCES

In economic theory, resources are defined generically as land, labour, or capital. In practical applications, it is only possible to measure resources approximately. Land consists of the 'indestructable powers of nature' and the mineral wealth embedded in the earth. Neither can be recovered on a realistic scale without the aid of capital and labour, so that it is not possible to determine the element of rent of land as a separate entity. Instead, we must fall back on an approach adopted by Vanek (1963, 10) in which resources are defined as the first measurable product of land. The product of iron mines is measured by the iron ore produced per year, and the value of different types of arable land is measured by the value of the wheat, milk, or logs produced. This is not as satisfactory as having values for the primal resources themselves, but it provides a means whereby one is able to identify the principal resources involved at various stages of processing. The point is illustrated in Table 1, which shows the percentage of the total of various resources used in production of each of eighty commodities. Unfortunately, it will be necessary to digress briefly before discussing this table in detail.

NOMENCLATURE

The analysis in the first section below is based on commodity data arranged according to a 125-level commodity code. These commodity classifications are an aggregation of a 644-level classification defined at Statistics Canada (15-501, 1961). The 125-level classes are defined in Table A1 of the appendix in terms of the Statistics Canada 644-level Commodity Code and in terms of the Canadian

Import Commodity Code. The reader should refer to this documentation for the exact definition of each 125-level class. The verbal name assigned to each class at the 125-level is at best a general indication of the commodities being classified. In some cases, two or more classes have the same verbal name. This is because they are distinguished, not so much by the general characteristics of the product classifications as by the level of processing or by the role the items were observed to play in international trade. The nature and motivation for the classification system is explained in the later sections.

The point to be stressed here is that the number assigned to each commodity class is the key to its identity. To illustrate: the 125-level class (52) is Cereal products. From Table A1 of the appendix it is quickly determined that Cereal products is an aggregation of commodity classes (95), (96), and (98) at the 644-level. One can determine (ibid.) that these 644-level classes are respectively, Breakfast cereal products, Biscuits, Ice cream cones, and Similar products and Other bakery products. The principal Import Commodity Code numbers are 06417, 06419, 06430, 06455, and 06499 etc. If the reader is so inclined, he may similarly determine the exact definition of any of the other 125-level commodity classifications by taking note of the number assigned to the class and referring to Table A1. In particular, he may determine the exact identity of the eighty commodities defined in Table 1.

USE OF RESOURCES IN EACH COMMODITY CLASSIFICATION

The columns of Table 1 are resource classifications. Each of these is an aggregation of resources of a particular kind at a fairly high level, and the exact content will not be obvious from the names. The detailed content of Agricultural resources, Forestry resources, Minerals and metals, and Energy resources are discussed in later sections. Column 7 is the sum of these five plus direct and indirect value added in fishing and may be regarded as an indication of the cost of land resources in the production of commodities. It is hoped that the first five names given in Table 1 are reasonably descriptive. Several resource classes in Table 1, however, require additional commentary.

The title for column 6 is Imported resources. These are sometimes referred to as Non-competing resources because there is no production in Canada. There are two columns in Table 1, columns 9 and 10, which report Other value added. Column 9 includes all the Other value added earned in the production of a commodity exclusive of wages and taxes. It may be regarded as a rough indication of the returns paid to owners of capital. Unfortunately, the magnitude also includes returns to land (rent) and some wages of management. In order to correct for the presence of the rent component in column 9, column

TABLE 1

Resources used in each of eighty commodities (percentage)

| NO. | NAME OF COMMODITY GROUP | TRADE/OUTPUT (1) | RESOURCES BASED ON LAND | | | | IMPORTED (6) | TOTAL (7) | LABOUR (8) | OTHER VALUE ADDED | |
			AGRICULTURAL (2)	FORESTRY (3)	MINING (4)	ENERGY (5)				INC.RES (9)	EXC.RES (10)
40.	SERVICES TO AGRICULTURE	.00	.15	.04	.02	.12	.04	.10	.06	.17	.18
41.	SERVICES TO MINING	.00	.06	.05	.12	.27	.06	.14	.34	.31	.36
42.	MEAT	-.00	21.07	.70	.46	1.81	1.19	7.60	1.67	2.47	.63
43.	MARGARINE AND SHORTENING	.01	1.67	.09	.06	.17	1.11	.62	.16	.23	.08
44.	HIDES AND SKINS	.14	.42	.01	.01	.04	.04	.15	.04	.05	.02
45.	CRUDE ANIMAL PRODUCTS	.06	.34	.01	.01	.03	.02	.12	.02	.04	.00
46.	POULTRY PROCESSED	-.02	3.19	.15	.07	.33	.13	1.17	.33	.45	.19
47.	DAIRY PRODUCTS	.01	17.27	.61	.36	1.54	1.13	6.23	1.17	1.87	.32
48.	FISH PRODUCTS	.58	.12	.13	.11	.23	.13	1.08	.29	.34	.07
49.	PROCESSED FOODS	-.24	5.99	.73	.65	1.11	12.81	2.53	1.38	1.53	1.15
50.	FEED MEAL AND FLOUR	.01	3.92	.19	.20	.48	1.11	1.52	.45	.57	.23
51.	WHEAT FLOUR,MALT STARCH	.15	5.21	.41	.19	.69	2.77	2.00	.76	.82	.39
52.	CEREAL PRODUCTS	-.03	.79	.31	.09	.30	1.76	.42	.44	.36	.34
53.	CONFECTIONARY PRODUCTS	-.05	.48	.17	.06	.15	3.17	.24	.23	.19	.17
54.	BEET, PULP AND SUGAR	.25	.09	.02	.01	.03	.56	.04	.03	.05	.05
55.	SUGAR REFINERY PRODUCTS	-.04	.45	.06	.04	.09	12.07	.19	.10	.16	.14
56.	LIQUOR AND BEER	.09	.91	.35	.20	.40	.41	.51	.58	.80	.87
57.	ALCOHOL AND WINE	-.43	.11	.02	.01	.02	.17	.05	.03	.04	.04
58.	TOBACCO, PROCESSED	.06	4.41	.49	.11	.42	.21	1.65	.46	.66	.31
59.	RUBBER PRODUCTS	-.08	.05	.05	.09	.16	2.34	.09	.22	.16	.19
60.	LEATHER	.04	.39	.03	.03	.09	.07	.17	.11	.08	.05
61.	RUBBER PRODUCTS	-.23	.06	.08	.16	.24	2.66	.14	.31	.26	.30
62.	LEATHER GOODS	-.12	.40	.15	.09	.21	.61	.24	.51	.22	.21
63.	TEXTILE PRODUCTS, COTTON	-.56	.07	.09	.06	.29	11.36	.14	.40	.25	.29
64.	YARN OF WOOL HAIR	-.22	.04	.01	.01	.03	.24	.03	.05	.03	.03
65.	TEXTILE PRODUCTS,WOOL	-.63	.20	.03	.03	.10	.63	.11	.16	.10	.09
66.	TEXTILES SILK AND SYNT.	-.17	.10	.19	.14	.36	1.09	.20	.43	.37	.43
67.	TEXTILE PRODUCTS N.E.S.,M	-.15	1.15	.46	.29	.88	8.59	.78	2.01	1.03	1.11

TABLE 1 continued

| NO. NAME OF COMMODITY GROUP | TRADE/OUTPUT (1) | RESOURCES BASED ON LAND | | | | IMPORTED (6) | TOTAL (7) | LABOUR (8) | OTHER VALUE ADDED | |
		AGRICULTURAL (2)	FORESTRY (3)	MINING (4)	ENERGY (5)				INC.RES (9)	EXC.RES (10)
68. TEXTILE PRODUCTS N.E.S.,M	-.21	.26	.23	.12	.35	2.63	.25	.70	.39	.44
69. FUR	-.00	.07	.02	.01	.04	.45	.04	.11	.05	.06
70. WOOD PRODUCTS,E	.41	.30	23.94	.21	.88	.25	3.73	1.54	.92	.47
71. WOOD PRODUCTS,M	-.02	.05	2.07	.07	.15	.08	.36	.26	.16	.13
72. WOOD PRODUCTS,M	-.03	.19	3.79	.43	.58	.91	.86	1.14	.66	.67
73. PULP AND PAPER PRODUCTS,E	.84	.42	22.93	1.12	3.79	.50	4.62	2.04	2.27	2.06
74. PULP AND PAPER PRODUCTS,M	-.11	.05	2.27	.12	.35	.08	.47	.25	.25	.23
75. PULP AND PAPER PRODUCTS,M	-.06	.27	7.28	.63	1.50	.47	1.71	1.43	1.20	1.20
76. PRINTING	-.21	.13	1.78	.25	.54	.21	.51	1.22	.73	.82
77. IRON AND STEEL INTERMED	-.18	.19	.30	3.97	1.84	.23	1.51	1.60	1.16	1.12
78. GRAPHITE AND CARBON	-.35	.01	.01	.31	.08	.01	.09	.04	.05	.04
79. IRON AND STEEL INTERMED,M	-.01	.18	.26	4.26	1.89	.23	1.57	1.45	1.14	1.07
80. IRON AND STEEL INTERMED,E	.50	.02	.03	.94	.35	.03	.32	.17	.17	.14
81. NONFERROUS METAL PROD.,E	.53	.21	.26	38.79	2.73	.24	8.93	2.03	2.82	.88
82. NONFERROUS METAL PROD.,M	-.19	.17	.30	3.46	1.00	.21	1.13	1.35	.96	.93
83. NONFERROUS METAL PROD.,E	.06	.03	.04	2.21	.23	.03	.54	.24	.23	.14
84. PLUMBING MISC.EQUIP.	-.45	.05	.09	.63	.27	.07	.25	.44	.27	.28
85. AGRICULTURAL MACHINERY	-.92	.03	.05	.25	.18	.08	.13	.32	.13	.14
86. OTHER MACHINERY AND EQUIP.	-.87	.18	.45	1.67	.85	.33	.74	1.48	.99	1.08
87. AIRCRAFT INC. PARTS	-.23	.07	.09	.46	.31	.15	.23	.82	.31	.33
88. AUTOS, TRUCKS AND PARTS	-.45	.34	.47	1.78	1.31	1.63	.96	2.29	1.71	1.94
89. BUSES AND LOCOMOTIVES	-.24	.01	.03	.08	.05	.04	.04	.09	.05	.06
90. TRANSPORTATION EQUIPMENT	-.12	.03	.08	.19	.15	.08	.11	.32	.14	.15
91. ELECTRICAL APPLIANCES	-.37	.21	.39	1.74	.90	.47	.77	1.90	1.01	1.10
92. ELECTRICAL EQUIPMENT	-.04	.07	.14	1.44	.29	.17	.43	.50	.39	.37
93. MINERAL PRODUCTS,E	.02	.13	.17	1.84	1.11	.18	.80	.71	.65	.67
94. MINERAL PRODUCTS,M	-.45	.08	.26	.93	.47	.26	.40	.51	.38	.39
95. PETROLEUM PRODUCTS,M	-.23	.02	.02	.04	1.24	.02	.42	.08	.18	.09

TABLE 1 continued

NO. NAME OF COMMODITY GROUP	TRADE/OUTPUT (1)	RESOURCES BASED ON LAND						LABOUR (8)	OTHER VALUE ADDED	
		AGRICULTURAL (2)	FORESTRY (3)	MINING (4)	ENERGY (5)	IMPORTED (6)	TOTAL (7)		INC.RES (9)	EXC.RES (10)
96. PETROLEUM PRODUCTS,M	-.09	.34	.25	.42	21.06	.32	7.03	1.13	2.71	1.12
97. NAPHTHA AND ASPHALT	-.09	.01	.01	.01	.56	.01	.22	.04	.09	.04
98. COAL PRODUCTS N.E.S.	-.40	.01	.02	.12	.14	.01	.08	.05	.07	.06
99. EXPLOSIVES	-.02	.02	.04	.10	.09	.05	.06	.13	.07	.07
100. PHARMACEUTICALS	-.13	.30	.27	.22	.33	.50	.29	.51	.46	.51
101. CHEMICALS	.19	.09	.12	.80	.79	.10	.47	.33	.42	.44
102. INORGANIC CHEMICALS,M	-.26	.68	.43	.98	1.23	.58	.88	.89	.94	.97
103. INORGANIC CHEMICALS,E	.03	.04	.04	.31	.35	.06	.19	.14	.19	.20
104. INDUSTRIAL CHEMICALS	-.15	.13	.16	.49	.69	.33	.39	.37	.47	.51
105. SCIENTIFIC EQUIPMENT	-.85	.03	.05	.21	.09	.05	.09	.20	.14	.16
106. JEWELRY	-1.00	.02	.04	.54	.08	.03	.15	.17	.12	.12
107. PLASTICS PRODUCTS	-.38	.12	.16	.12	.19	.20	.15	.21	.17	.18
108. END PRODUCTS N.E.S.,M	-.35	.10	.37	.23	.25	.43	.21	.46	.31	.34
109. END PRODUCTS N.E.S.,M	-.21	.03	.06	.11	.07	.05	.06	.10	.07	.08
110. DRESSING AND DYEING	.00	.01	.01	.01	.04	.02	.02	.05	.03	.03
111. CONSTRUCTION	.00	2.22	12.86	13.99	7.98	3.05	7.94	14.24	8.21	8.52
112. TRANSPORTATION-TRADE	.03	9.73	3.78	2.71	10.93	5.01	7.78	18.65	16.24	18.46
113. ELECTRIC POWER	.01	.09	.26	.43	9.38	.09	3.18	1.02	3.04	3.76
114. WATER SERVICES	-.00	.00	.03	.00	.02	.00	.01	.02	.02	.02
115. COMMUNICATIONS	.01	.14	.16	.15	.33	.13	.21	1.89	1.93	2.39
116. BUSINESS SERVICE	-.01	7.95	2.74	2.33	4.56	6.85	4.96	10.35	19.82	23.61
117. PERSONAL SERVICE	-.06	.45	.43	.53	1.29	.89	.73	2.38	3.47	4.21
118. ADVERTISING,TRAVEL	-.00	.87	1.77	.48	1.60	.92	1.15	2.34	2.50	2.87
119. REPAIR, SUPPLIES, SERVICE	.09	3.74	2.55	3.07	4.22	4.02	3.57	6.58	5.55	6.09

10 was prepared. Rent arising from the use of land resources, including mining, is an unknown magnitude, but we do know that it accrues as part of the value added in the resource industries. The magnitude in column 9 includes all of the Other value added earned directly or indirectly in production. It includes not only the amount earned in the industries producing commodities, but also the amount of value added earned in the industries which supply intermediate goods or resources to these industries directly and indirectly. In column 10, the value added of the resource industries is excluded. The magnitudes in column 10 therefore exclude a little too much. They exclude not only rent to land in agriculture and mining as intended but also returns to capital in the resource industries.

Table 1 was prepared in order to give the reader an initial impression of the direct plus indirect use of resources by commodities. The magnitudes in the table refer to the productive use of each of the commodities expressed as a percentage of total productive use in the economy as a whole. The reader can verify that 39 per cent of mining resources were used by Non-ferrous metal products (81). Table 1 also indicates the trade orientation of each of the commodity groups. Column 1 indicates the ratio of trade to output. The Non-ferrous metal products (81) classification exported 0.53 of its output. The table reveals even at this level of aggregation that each resource is closely identified with only a few commodities. This identification becomes even more marked if we consider a lower level of resource classification.

In Table A2 of the appendix, resource flows are displayed for the same commodity classifications as Table 1 but there are 39 columns reporting on resource use by commodity. By referring to the appendix the reader can determine, for example, that in 1961 Non-ferrous metal products (81) used approximately 84 per cent of the Metal ores (22) processed in Canada and 85 per cent of Radioactive ores (23). It is even more apparent in Table A2 than in Table 1 that the flow of each resource is easily identified with one or a few commodities.

It is also apparent from Table A2 that land resources do not generally require other land resources as inputs. The last row of Table A2 indicates the percentage of resources used by the resource industries themselves. Most of these percentages are very small, but there are exceptions. Other grain (4), Hay and grass (10), Other crude wood (19), Peat moss (34), and Abrasives (36) supply more than 10 per cent of their output to the other resource classifications; 95 per cent of Custom forestry (20) output is shipped to other resource categories. These five resource categories, however, are exceptions to the general rule that resource commodities are the first measurable product of land produced without the use of the other land-based resources. The principal exception is found in the resource classifications which use land to produce products from live animals or which supply live animals to processers. These classifications use most of the grain, hay, and wood which is supplied by one land-based resource classification to another.

There is another point that can be made in connection with Table A2. At a later stage we shall suggest that the degree-of-processing concept is rather vague and ambiguous. Table A2 shows that some resource products in agriculture qualify immediately as end products. These can be quickly identified if the reader will refer to row 116 of Table A2 (which includes retail trade). 72 per cent of Eggs (6), 33 per cent of Honey and beeswax (7), and 29 per cent of Nuts, fruits and berries (8), and 28 per cent of Vegetables (9) are shipped directly to retail trade. Although the resource commodities shipped directly to retail trade qualify as end products, they would not be considered highly processed ones. Such cases illustrate the dangers inherent in formulating policy in these terms.

The column headings of Table 1 and of Table A2 respectively define resources at the level of aggregation and disaggregation adopted in this study. In the following chapters these definitions are related to such matters as processing, trade and tariffs.

2
Resources and commodity trade: the Canadian experience

This chapter is an empirical study of the relationship between Canada's resources and her commodity trade. The concepts introduced in the previous chapter are applied, first to data at a high level of aggregation and then to data aggregated to a more detailed 125-level classification. In the final sections, Canada's trade figures for a number of different years are compared, followed, by a comparison of differences in trade in resources and commodities by region.

EMPIRICAL RESULTS FROM AGGREGATED DATA

The nine resource classifications listed in the left-hand column of Table 2 are the same as those listed as column headings in Table 1. The information in the body of the table reports on various aspects of trade in these resources. For example, line 1A refers to Agricultural resources exported or imported without further processing. These consist, therefore, almost entirely of actual resource flows and should be distinguished from line 1B. The item on line 1B, column 1, is not an actual resource flow but rather an estimate of the direct plus indirect value of the resources required to produce commodity exports. Similarly, the item on line 1B in column 2 is the direct plus indirect cost of the resources required to produce Canadian imports had these imports been produced in Canada. This distinction between lines marked A and B in Table 2 holds throughout, with a minor exception. It sometimes takes resources to produce other resources. Hay is fed to live animals, for example, and, since both hay and live animals are Agricultural resources, the hay used to feed exported live animals is counted on line A.

To illustrate the interpretation of the figures in Table 2 for each of the resource classifications, let us continue with consideration of the case of Agricultural resources. On line 1A, the reader will find the value of the 1961 trade in unprocessed Agricultural resources. In 1961, Canada exported $883.9 million of Agricultural resources and imported −$282.17 million. This is determined by reading under column 1 and column 2 of Table 2 on line 1A. In column 3, the reader finds the figure 0.52. This is an index of the direction of trade computed as follows:

$$\text{Index} = (\text{Exports} - \text{Imports}) / (\text{Imports} + \text{Exports}). \tag{1}$$

This index is equal to +1 if Canada exports Agricultural resources but does not import, and to −1 if Canada imports Agricultural resources but does not export. If imports equal exports, the index is zero. Since in the case of Agricultural resources the index is approximately 0.5, exports are three times the value of imports.[1]

Line 1B of Table 2 refers to the value of the Agricultural resources that would be required to produce Canadian exports or imports. On line 1B we note that $171.2 million of Agricultural resources are required to produce the processed commodities exported from Canada. With regard to commodities imported, Table 2 indicates it would require −$190.72 million worth of Agricultural resources to produce these in Canada. From inspection of line 1A, we learned that Canada was a net exporter of Agricultural resources in 1961. From line 1B, we learn that Canada was a net importer of Agricultural resources as part of the value of processed goods. The commodities Canada exported required less Agricultural resources to produce than would the commodities Canada imported, had these been produced in Canada.

Agricultural resources may also be used to illustrate the interpretation of calculations appearing on lines denoted as C in Table 2. The number appearing on line 1C under column 1 is used to compare the value of Agricultural resources exported in unprocessed form to the value of the Agricultural resources required to produce the processed commodities exported from Canada. The index is the same as used in equation 1 above:

$$\text{Index} = (\text{Line A} - \text{Line B}) / (\text{Line A} + \text{Line B}). \tag{2}$$

1 We could, of course, use an alternate index, such as imports divided by exports or exports divided by imports. The problem with these is that they will become exceedingly large and approach infinity when the denominator approaches zero. The interested reader can convert the value of the index, if he chooses. Use the formula:
Exports / Imports = (1 + Index) / (1 − Index).

TABLE 2

Resources required to produce Canadian imports and exports, 1961, 1969, and average 1967-9

	1961 EXPORTS	1961 IMPORTS	1961 DIRECTION	AVERAGE 1967-1969 EXPORTS	AVERAGE 1967-1969 IMPORTS	AVERAGE 1967-1969 DIRECTION	1969 EXPORTS	1969 IMPORTS	1969 DIRECTION
1. AGRICULTURAL RESOURCE COSTS									
A. CHARGED TO RESOURCE TRADE	883.90	-282.17	.52	913.75	-429.31	.36	747.36	-458.15	.24
B. CHARGED TO COMMODITY TRADE	171.20	-190.72	.05	272.57	-327.26	-.09	300.19	-383.43	-.12
C. (A-B)/(A+B)	.68	.19		.54	.13		.43	.09	
2. FORESTRY RESOURCES									
A. CHARGED TO RESOURCE TRADE	56.22	-19.30	.49	67.04	-40.56	.25	62.17	-41.42	.20
B. CHARGED TO COMMODITY TRADE	468.26	-93.84	.67	794.08	-172.18	.64	895.21	-197.96	.64
C. (A-B)/(A+B)	-.79	-.66		-.84	-.62		-.87	-.65	
3. MINERALS AND METALS									
A. CHARGED TO RESOURCE TRADE	746.87	-200.48	.58	1,068.10	-315.27	.54	1,097.16	-309.97	.56
B. CHARGED TO COMMODITY TRADE	570.20	-249.96	.39	1,072.42	-577.54	.30	1,121.74	-664.22	.26
C. (A-B)/(A+B)	.13	-.11		.00	-.29		-.01	-.36	
4. ENERGY RESOURCES									
A. CHARGED TO RESOURCE TRADE	308.04	-523.50	-.26	741.43	-796.09	-.04	824.64	-762.30	.04
B. CHARGED TO COMMODITY TRADE	279.53	-319.08	-.07	553.30	-661.60	-.09	627.20	-742.83	-.08
C. (A-B)/(A+B)	.05	.24		.15	.09		.14	.01	
5. NON-COMPETING RESOURCES									
A. CHARGED TO RESOURCE TRADE	3.73	-617.39	-.99	6.27	-766.35	-.98	6.02	-809.12	-.99
B. CHARGED TO COMMODITY TRADE	21.24	-89.83	-.62	51.82	-140.73	-.46	60.19	-155.37	-.44
C. (A-B)/(A+B)	-.70	.75		-.78	.69		-.82	.68	
6. TOTAL ALL RESOURCES									
A. CHARGED TO RESOURCE TRADE	1,996.79	-1,334.10	.20	2,793.60	-1,964.53	.17	2,734.54	-1,976.59	.16
B. CHARGED TO COMMODITY TRADE	1,555.03	-865.64	.28	2,794.09	-1,753.52	.23	3,052.95	-2,005.29	.21
C. (A-B)/(A+B)	.12	.21		-.00	.06		-.06	-.01	
7. WAGES									
A. CHARGED TO RESOURCE TRADE	609.10	-339.37	.28	849.50	-549.19	.21	834.47	-526.44	.23
B. CHARGED TO COMMODITY TRADE	2,408.79	-3,251.93	-.15	5,340.24	-7,164.89	-.15	6,211.89	-8,201.18	-.14
C. (A-B)/(A+B)	-.60	-.81		-.73	-.86		-.76	-.88	
8. OTHER VALUE ADDED									
A. CHARGED TO RESOURCE TRADE	1,072.61	-569.24	.31	1,586.07	-876.43	.29	1,568.06	-880.76	.28
B. CHARGED TO COMMODITY TRADE	1,911.59	-2,033.12	-.03	3,782.66	-4,245.70	-.06	4,322.71	-4,880.10	-.06
C. (A-B)/(A+B)	-.28	-.56		-.41	-.66		-.47	-.69	
9. OTHER VALUE ADDED EXCLUDING INDIRECT RESOURCE VALUE ADDED									
A. CHARGED TO RESOURCE TRADE	962.66	-536.49	.28	1,483.08	-826.04	.28	1,476.36	-828.53	.28
B. CHARGED TO COMMODITY TRADE	1,167.02	-1,603.78	-.16	2,452.43	-3,388.08	-.16	2,885.57	-3,899.63	-.15
C. (A-B)/(A+B)	-.10	-.50		-.25	-.61		-.32	-.65	

*EXPORTS AND IMPORTS ARE EXPRESSED IN MILLIONS OF DOLLARS.

If the value of Agricultural resources exported directly in resource form exceeds the value of Agricultural resources exported as part of the value of exported commodities, the figure on line C will be positive. In the event that Agricultural resources are exported but none are used to produce exported commodities, the index will equal 1. The index will be negative unity in the event that there are no exports of Agricultural resources, but there is some use of them in production of exported commodities. Since, in fact, the index is 0.68, we conclude that the value of Agricultural resources used to produce exported commodities is less than the value exported in unprocessed form.

This last observation should be compared to column 2, line 1C, which reports a similar computation for Imports (We are referring, of course, to the sum or difference of positive numbers). This figure is 0.19, indicating that the value of Agricultural resources which would be required to produce Canadian imports is less than the value of unprocessed Agricultural resources imported. Since 0.68 is greater than 0.19, we conclude that imports are relatively more processed than exports.

INTERPRETATION OF AGGREGATED DATA

Lines 6, 7, 8, and 9 of Table 2 suggest the hypothesis that Canadian comparative advantage lies in the abundance of resources relative to other factors of production. From lines 7B and 8B in column 3, it is determined that the amount of Wages and Other value added that would be required for Canada to produce her own 1961 commodity imports would exceed the amount of Wages and Other value added required to produce Canadian exports. Canadian imports of commodities are intensive in Wages and Other value added. From line 6B it can be determined that the value of the resources required to produce Canadian exports exceeds the value of the resources required to produce her own imports. Canadian exports are resource-intensive. These data underestimate the actual extent to which Canadian imports are intensive in Wages and Other value added relative to exports because they do not take into consideration the amount of Wages and Other value added exported as part of the value of unprocessed resources.

From line 6A, column 3, the reader can verify that Canada is a net exporter of unprocessed resources in 1961. The net export of resources in unprocessed form carries with it a net export of Wages (line 7A, column 3) and of Other value added (line 8A, column 3) as part of the cost of producing the exported resources. Wages and Other value added in this case are exported because Canada is abundant in resources.

This point can also be established in connection with the data on line 9B, column 3, in Table 2. In the computations shown on these lines, the Other value added in the resource industries is excluded. Without this, Canada appears to have a higher import displacement of Other value added than when it is present. A significant proportion of the exports of Other value added through commodity trade consists of the value required to produce resources, which in this interpretation is exported because resources are abundant. After making allowance for the necessity of exporting Other value added through direct export along with resources, we determine that Canada is more distinctly displacing Other value added through commodity imports.

The data for 1961 imply that Canada has a comparative advantage in producing commodities which require relatively large expenditures, directly and indirectly, on resources. It will therefore be of some interest to study the trade pattern with respect to particular resource commodities to determine if these display the pattern noted in the case of resources in general. A net export of a resource would carry with it the implication that Canada was abundant in that resource relative to the rest of the world, and if we find that there is also a net export through commodity trade this would support the hypothesis that the excess supply of the resource had accounted for a source of comparative advantage in Canadian commodity trade. One might then search for particular commodities which appear to require this resource relatively more than other commodities. Through this line of logic, one could begin to identify some commodity groups in which foreign tariff reductions would shift output in Canada in the direction of comparative advantage.

A similar logic can be applied in reverse to the Canadian tariff. If there are resources imported in unprocessed form into Canada, and if these resources are imported as part of the cost of commodities, one may hypothesize that the commodities using relatively large amounts of such imported resources are produced in Canada at a comparative disadvantage. These then would be cases where a reduction in the Canadian producers who presently purchase intermediate goods at the high tariff-protected Canadian price would have the opportunity to purchase at the cheaper world price, and consumers would benefit from the lower price of end products.

RECENT EVIDENCE ON COMPARATIVE COSTS

The underlying hypothesis of this study — that Canadian natural resources are an important factor determining Canada's comparative advantage in commodity trade — has received corroboration in a study by Postner (1975), published while this manuscript was in press. Evidence was presented in Table 2 above that Canadian commodity trade is essentially an exchange in which wages and Other value added imported exceeds the value of these items exported, while the value of resources imported through commodity trade is less than the value of resources required to produce exports. Postner's research is designed to investigate the relationship between Canada's commodity trade, resource base, and comparative advantage. The reader will find evidence in this study that Canada's comparative advantage in commodity trade is based on a relative abundance of natural resources.

Postner's study examines the role of capital and labour in greater detail than can be found in the earlier literature. Principal results relating to this study can be found in his Table II. If measured in units of wages and salaries, Canada is an importer of labour through commodity trade. This is true of both simple labour and 'human capital.' Measured in units of man-hours, however, Canada was an exporter through commodity trade in 1961 (but shifted to import status by 1971). The data suggest that, at least in part, Canada's imports of labour through commodities arises because the commodities Canada imports are produced from high-wage labour while the commodities Canada exports are produced from low-wage labour. Postner produces further detail on this point. Measured in man-years, Canada exports Elementary Labour through commodity trade but imports High School and University Labour. Judging from the 1971 data, however, this condition appears to be reversing.

Postner's results also indicate that Canada is a net exporter of Gross Structures and Gross Machinery through commodity trade in 1961 (and 1970). Since the calculations of Table 1 above indicate a net import of Other value added through commodity trade, and given Postner's results, it would appear that this arises because profits are higher in Canada's import-competing sector. This is an important matter for future research but it has no direct bearing on the objectives of the present study, which is concerned with the natural resource basis of Canada's trade. In this respect, Postner's study provides convincing corroboration of our Table 2, which indicates that natural resources are an important source of Canada's comparative advantage. It is an objective in the present study to examine the implications of this in detail.[2]

DATA FOR RESOURCE SUBCLASSES 1961

From inspection of Table 2, it is already apparent that some resource subcategories do not correspond to the pattern illustrated by Total all resources. Either the resource is not exported from Canada or, though exported in

2 'It is claimed that by 1970 the prime source of Canadian comparative advantage was her factor endowment of nonrenewable resources. On the other hand, we are much less confident regarding the factor sources of Canadian disadvantage in international trade' (Postner, 1975, 40).

unprocessed form, it is not exported as part of the value of processed commodities. Two classes of resource follow the pattern of Total all resources. Both Minerals and metals and Forestry products are exported in unprocessed form and as part of the cost of processed commodities. This would be consistent with the hypothesis that a Canadian comparative advantage has been established at higher levels of processing, based on resource abundance in Minerals and metals and Forestry resources.

Energy resources and Non-competing resources are classifications in which resources are imported in unprocessed form and also imported as part of the value of commodities in 1961. By the end of the decade, however, Energy was a net export in unprocessed form, and after this change only Non-competing resources follow the pattern, with both imports of the unprocessed resource and imports through the value of commodities. This case is consistent with the hypothesis that Canada has a comparative disadvantage in producing commodities which are intensive in the use of such resources as Raw cotton, Wool in the grease, Coffee, and Tea. If the hypothesis is correct, and if it is possible in the long run to shift capital and employment out of such production and into more efficient industries, present levels of tariff and non-tariff barriers should be reduced in the long run through negotiations aimed at foreign tariff reduction in lines where there is a Canadian comparative advantage.

Agricultural resources are exported from Canada, but are also imported as part of the value of processed commodities. This is also true of Energy by the year 1969. Such a pattern is inconsistent with the hypothesis that resources establish comparative advantage in later stages of processing, and it will be necessary to return to this when these resources and commodity groups are studied at a more disaggregated level.

A final comment should be made concerning the lines denoted by C in Table 2. In most cases, both imports and exports are dominated by unprocessed flows, as in the case of Agricultural resources, Energy, and Total all resources. Only in the case of Forestry resources do we have a dominance of trade as part of the value of commodities. As one would expect, exports are relatively more in the form of unprocessed resources and imports more in processed form.

TRADE DATA FOR LATER YEARS

In the second and third set of columns of Table 2, results are displayed for the years 1967-9 and for the single year 1969. The data are based on the 1961 input-output matrix and in effect assume that the 1961 proportions of intermediate goods and resources required per unit of output are also appropriate for the later periods. In the technical language of economics, it is assumed that there are no external economies, economies of scale, or substitutions in production in the time period under study. Despite these restrictive assumptions, the resulting calculations have a useful interpretation. By using trade vectors of the later years with the production coefficients for 1961, one can determine the robustness of the 1961 results with regard to changes in the trade pattern. The trade vectors of the later years represent alternate patterns of exports and imports, all of which are within the expected range of observation in Canada under changing world conditions.

The data for later years in Table 2 are also an indication of the actual relationship between resources and trade for those years. They would constitute a more reliable estimate, however, if they had been computed from the actual input-output coefficients of the later years. Unfortunately, such data were not available when the computations for this study were prepared. One therefore must consider the possible impact discussed above in connection with the criticisms of the Heckscher-Ohlin Theorem, that the rank order of resource use by commodity may have changed over the eight-year period considered. Evidence indicates that this is not likely to affect our conclusions.

An encouraging source of evidence is the empirical work cited in chapter 1, which indicates that reversals of factor intensities are not likely to occur. If commodity 1 uses relatively more labour than commodity 2, this will also hold over the expected range of relative resource prices. In addition, one should cite the work of Weiser (1968), who shows that the structural changes in US input-output coefficients were not great enough to alter the relative amount of capital and labour services required by imports and exports over the eleven-year period 1947 to 1958. It should be noted that this period includes the substantial changes following recovery from the second world war. Working with Canadian data, Postner (1975, 17) reaches a similar conclusion.

More relevant, as far as Canadian data are concerned, is Table A2 of the appendix, which was discussed at the end of chapter 1. The reader will recall that the columns of this table display the percentage of total use (thirty-nine resources) by each of eighty commodity classes. It may be verified from inspection of this table that, in a typical case, nearly all of each resource disappears in the production of one or a few commodities. There is very little scope for changes in the pattern of resource use by commodity.

In part because of the impact of inflation, the levels of import and export figures are much higher in 1969 than in 1961. However, the indices displayed in the table are pure numbers independent of inflationary trend. These indices (shown on lines C and under the column headed Direction) are similar in the two years in that, except for Energy, there are no changes in sign. The pattern of trade in resources as described for 1961 is essentially correct for the later years considered.

Although the calculations based on the trade vectors of later years would suggest that the pattern of resource use does not change qualitatively, there are certain notable trends over time. In particular, one notes from Table 2 that, except for Energy, there is a general increase in the resources traded as part of the value of commodities, compared to the amount shipped in the form of unprocessed resources. On any of the lines marked C the reader will find that the index under an export column or import column is becoming algebraically smaller. For Total all resources it has shifted from 0.12 and 0.21 in 1961 to -0.06 and -0.01 by 1969. It would appear that increasingly the effects of trade on the supply and demand for resources will operate as a demand derived from trade in processed commodities rather than as direct resource demand. If so, commodity trade will increasingly reflect the resource endowments of the nations trading, and Canada will need to secure channels of trade in commodities which serve the function of balancing her resource abundance and scarcity. If we operate under the hypothesis that resource abundance is an important determinant of comparative advantage, such a strategy will also move Canada in the direction of her comparative advantage, and hence toward greater per capita income.

TRADE WITH VARIOUS REGIONS

The question must be considered whether or not the characteristics of trade we observed in Canada's relationship with the world as a whole also characterize Canada's trade with particular regions. Regional trade figures are displayed in Tables 3 and 4. Table 3 reports on trade for the year 1969. In Table 4, trade figures are displayed for the average of 1967, 1968, and 1969. A review of these tables will reveal differences by region in Canada's trade in unprocessed resources and in her trade in resources as part of the value of commodities.

In trade with the United States, Canada is a net importer of both Agricultural resources shipped in unprocessed form and those shipped as part of the value of commodities. This is exactly opposite to Canada's relationship with the United Kingdom and Japan, where Canada is a net exporter of agricultural resources in unprocessed form and as part of the value of commodities. In trade with the EEC, Canada appears to have an exportable surplus at the resource stage, but this is reversed when we examine the data on resources traded as part of the value of commodities.

In trade with the world as a whole, Canada has a surplus of unprocessed Forestry resources and also exports more than she imports as part of the value of commodities. This is true of Canada's trade with each region except that, in trade with the United States, Canada's trade in resources is balanced.

TABLE 3

Resources required to produce Canadian commodity imports from and exports to US, EEC, UK, and Japan, 1969

	UNITED STATES			E.E.C.			UNITED KINGDOM			JAPAN		
	EXPORTS	IMPORTS	DIRECTION	EXPORTS	IMPORTS	DIRECTION	EXPORTS	IMPORTS	DIRECTION	EXPORTS	IMPORTS	DIRECTION
1. AGRICULTURAL RESOURCES												
A. CHARGED TO RESOURCE TRADE	129.29	-387.16	-.50	129.33	-7.68	.89	122.50	-3.58	.94	124.79	-.28	1.00
B. CHARGED TO COMMODITY TRADE	160.66	-210.68	-.13	12.95	-31.35	-.42	55.80	-26.92	.35	11.50	-9.35	.10
C. (A-B)/(A+B)	-.11	.30		.82	-.61		.37	-.77		.83	-.94	
2. FORESTRY RESOURCES												
A. CHARGED TO RESOURCE TRADE	39.22	-39.54	-.00	7.59	-.06	.98	2.77	-.07	.95	9.20	-.01	1.00
B. CHARGED TO COMMODITY TRADE	681.37	-144.56	.65	46.98	-9.59	.66	64.11	-9.03	.75	37.32	-10.89	.55
C. (A-B)/(A+B)	-.89	-.57		-.72	-.99		-.92	-.99		-.60	-1.00	
3. MINERALS AND METALS												
A. CHARGED TO RESOURCE TRADE	433.81	-163.34	.45	199.39	-1.92	.98	119.60	-4.78	.92	203.07	-.02	1.00
B. CHARGED TO COMMODITY TRADE	633.58	-495.71	.12	88.91	-39.96	.38	189.08	-44.05	.62	51.82	-29.51	.27
C. (A-B)/(A+B)	-.19	-.50		.38	-.91		-.23	-.80		.59	-1.00	
4. ENERGY RESOURCES												
A. CHARGED TO RESOURCE TRADE	753.23	-258.19	.49	16.12	-.59	.93	13.07	-.45	.93	21.82	-.07	.99
B. CHARGED TO COMMODITY TRADE	459.76	-473.47	-.01	29.51	-43.08	-.19	49.84	-37.86	.14	21.45	-24.76	-.07
C. (A-B)/(A+B)	.24	-.29		-.29	-.97		-.58	-.98		.01	-.99	
5. NON-COMPETING RESOURCES												
A. CHARGED TO RESOURCE TRADE	3.46	-227.02	-.97	.62	-.58	.03	.52	-.34	.21	.53	-7.69	-.87
B. CHARGED TO COMMODITY TRADE	40.80	-89.56	-.37	2.04	-11.33	-.69	6.90	-12.48	-.29	.89	-9.03	-.82
C. (A-B)/(A+B)	-.84	.43		-.54	-.90		-.86	-.95		-.25	-.08	
6. TOTAL ALL RESOURCES												
A. CHARGED TO RESOURCE TRADE	1,357.39	-961.96	.17	352.80	-10.55	.94	258.25	-9.06	.93	359.09	-4.24	.98
B. CHARGED TO COMMODITY TRADE	2,010.20	-1,332.93	.20	182.46	-125.06	.19	372.56	-118.49	.52	123.25	-78.17	.22
C. (A-B)/(A+B)	-.19	-.16		.32	-.84		-.18	-.86		.49	-.90	
7. WAGES												
A. CHARGED TO RESOURCE TRADE	411.43	-336.56	.10	144.63	-3.10	.95	84.38	-3.38	.92	112.02	-.47	.99
B. CHARGED TO COMMODITY TRADE	4,759.14	-6,170.47	-.13	244.43	-518.98	-.36	409.14	-533.73	-.13	136.18	-346.02	-.44
C. (A-B)/(A+B)	-.84	-.90		-.36	-.99		-.66	-.99		-.10	-1.00	
8. OTHER VALUE ADDED												
A. CHARGED TO RESOURCE TRADE	800.82	-430.68	.30	195.56	-5.65	.94	137.40	-4.61	.94	201.85	-1.05	.99
B. CHARGED TO COMMODITY TRADE	3,172.33	-3,579.14	-.06	194.29	-314.81	.24	361.42	-305.60	.08	119.18	-190.83	-.23
C. (A-B)/(A+B)	-.60	-.79		.00	-.96		-.45	-.97		.26	-.99	
9. OTHER VALUED ADDED EXCLUDING INDIRECT RESOURCE VALUE ADDED												
A. CHARGED TO RESOURCE TRADE	770.65	-390.40	.33	181.32	-4.95	.95	123.09	-4.22	.93	188.89	-.99	.99
B. CHARGED TO COMMODITY TRADE	2,270.79	-2,954.11	-.13	104.58	-253.84	-.42	162.48	-248.51	-.21	59.18	-154.92	-.45
C. (A-B)/(A+B)	-.49	-.77		.27	-.96		-.14	-.97		.52	-.99	

* Exports and Imports are expressed in millions of dollars.

TABLE 4

Resources required to produce Canadian commodity imports from and exports to US, EEC, UK, and Japan, 1967, 1968, and average 1969

	UNITED STATES			E.E.C.			UNITED KINGDOM			JAPAN		
	EXPORTS	IMPORTS	DIRECTION	EXPORTS	IMPORTS	DIRECTION	EXPORTS	IMPORTS	DIRECTION	EXPORTS	IMPORTS	DIRECTION
1. AGRICULTURAL RESOURCE COSTS												
A. CHARGED TO RESOURCE TRADE	126.83	-367.07	-.49	144.95	-6.72	.91	139.53	-3.44	.95	146.65	-.26	1.00
B. CHARGED TO COMMODITY TRADE	138.23	-183.16	-.14	13.07	-28.16	-.37	55.94	-24.75	.39	8.75	-7.71	.06
C. (A-B)/(A+B)	-.04	.33		.83	-.61		.43	-.76		.89	-.93	
2. FORESTRY RESOURCES												
A. CHARGED TO RESOURCE TRADE	38.99	-38.74	.00	7.15	-.08	.98	3.57	-.06	.97	13.05	-.01	1.00
B. CHARGED TO COMMODITY TRADE	597.26	-125.89	.65	39.25	-8.73	.64	67.92	-8.08	.79	33.24	-8.88	.58
C. (A-B)/(A+B)	-.88	-.53		-.69	-.98		-.90	-.99		-.44	-1.00	
3. MINERALS AND METALS												
A. CHARGED TO RESOURCE TRADE	453.24	-184.64	.42	170.57	-2.00	.98	129.41	-4.65	.93	175.08	-.06	1.00
B. CHARGED TO COMMODITY TRADE	596.51	-427.94	.16	73.42	-36.72	.33	206.47	-41.83	.66	51.18	-23.39	.37
C. (A-B)/(A+B)	-.14	-.40		.40	-.90		-.23	-.80		.55	-1.00	
4. ENERGY RESOURCES												
A. CHARGED TO RESOURCE TRADE	657.82	-320.66	.34	15.75	-.53	.93	14.48	-.47	.94	26.64	-.08	.99
B. CHARGED TO COMMODITY TRADE	396.82	-415.96	-.02	25.26	-37.54	-.20	51.55	-36.42	.17	18.48	-19.63	-.03
C. (A-B)/(A+B)	.25	-.13		-.23	-.97		-.56	-.97		.18	-.99	
5. NON-COMPETING RESOURCES												
A. CHARGED TO RESOURCE TRADE	3.26	-229.25	-.97	.64	-.84	-.13	.57	-.22	.44	.59	-7.98	-.86
B. CHARGED TO COMMODITY TRADE	32.93	-79.61	-.41	1.74	-10.23	-.71	7.45	-11.65	-.22	.83	-8.18	-.82
C. (A-B)/(A+B)	-.82	.48		-.46	-.85		-.86	-.96		-.17	-.01	
6. TOTAL ALL RESOURCES												
A. CHARGED TO RESOURCE TRADE	1,278.63	-1,025.87	.11	338.78	-9.76	.94	287.32	-8.73	.94	361.66	-4.42	.98
B. CHARGED TO COMMODITY TRADE	1,795.67	-1,159.81	.22	155.25	-112.11	.16	395.39	-111.69	.56	113.22	-62.98	.29
C. (A-B)/(A+B)	-.17	-.06		.37	-.84		-.16	-.85		.52	-.87	
7. WAGES												
A. CHARGED TO RESOURCE TRADE	398.66	-373.32	.03	107.40	-2.89	.95	92.18	-3.14	.93	112.47	-.57	.99
B. CHARGED TO COMMODITY TRADE	3,971.81	-5,398.09	-.15	206.35	-458.80	-.38	427.07	-485.14	-.06	123.08	-271.55	-.38
C. (A-B)/(A+B)	-.82	-.87		-.32	-.99		-.64	-.99		-.05	-1.00	
8. OTHER VALUE ADDED												
A. CHARGED TO RESOURCE TRADE	741.98	-458.72	.24	188.29	-5.10	.95	153.48	-4.39	.94	201.15	-1.25	.99
B. CHARGED TO COMMODITY TRADE	2,694.56	-3,110.72	.07	166.31	-276.23	-.25	376.02	-278.94	.15	106.66	-149.86	-.17
C. (A-B)/(A+B)	-.57	-.74		.06	-.96		-.42	-.97		.31	-.98	
9. OTHER VALUE ADDED EXCLUDING INDIRECT RESOURCE VALUE ADDED												
A. CHARGED TO RESOURCE TRADE	711.79	-419.20	.26	173.98	-4.48	.95	137.08	-4.01	.94	187.08	-1.18	.99
B. CHARGED TO COMMODITY TRADE	1,881.02	-2,567.48	-.15	89.49	-221.67	-.42	164.47	-224.56	-.15	50.97	-120.83	-.41
C. (A-B)/(A+B)	-.45	-.72		.32	-.96		-.09	-.96		.57	-.98	

*EXPORTS AND IMPORTS ARE EXPRESSED IN MILLIONS OF DOLLARS.

TABLE 5

Direct and indirect trade in thirty-nine resources – average 1967-9

NO. NAME OF CLASSIFICATION	PERCENTAGE OF TOTAL RESOURCE EXPORTS (1)	INDIRECT RESOURCE IMPORTS (2)	INDEX OF TRADE THROUGH COMMODITIES (3)	RATIO: INDIRECT SHIPMENTS TO DIRECT SHIPMENTS (4)	INDEX OF RESOURCE TRADE (5)
1. LIVE ANIMALS	.046	-.098	-.122	2.222	.417
3. WHEAT	.014	-.012	.318	.063	1.000
4. OTHER GRAIN	.010	-.017	-.007	.529	.041
5. MILK	.012	-.019	.030	R	I
6. EGGS	.001	-.002	-.141	2.353	-.758
7. HONEY AND BEESWAX	.000	-.000	-.234	.286	.339
8. NUTS, FRUITS, BERRIES	.002	-.010	-.439	.350	-.629
9. VEGETABLES	.005	-.017	-.394	.667	-.766
10. HAY, GRASS AND NURSERY	.002	-.002	.120	.305	-.270
11. OIL SEED OIL NUTS	.005	-.023	-.449	.151	.161
12. HOPS	.000	-.000	.333	.927	-.299
13. TOBACCO	.009	-.004	.569	R	I
14. FUR	.001	-.006	-.528	.095	.176
15. WOOL IN THE GREASE	.001	-.006	-.536	3.955	-.605
16. LOGS AND BOLTS	.124	-.049	.518	21.803	-.298
17. POLES AND PIT PROPS	.001	-.002	-.037	.385	.791
18. PULPWOOD	.158	-.050	.680	17.036	.762
19. OTHER CRUDE WOOD	.001	-.001	-.005	.302	.958
20. CUSTOM FORESTRY	.034	-.013	.637	R	I
21. FISH LANDINGS	.041	-.010	.744	2.002	.392
22. METAL ORES	.334	-.222	.432	2.329	.371
23. RADIO-ACTIVE ORES	.038	-.025	.441	3.827	1.000

TABLE 5 continued

NO.	NAME OF CLASSIFICATION	PERCENTAGE OF TOTAL INDIRECT RESOURCE EXPORTS (1)	PERCENTAGE OF TOTAL INDIRECT RESOURCE IMPORTS (2)	INDEX OF TRADE THROUGH COMMODITIES (3)	RATIO: INDIRECT SHIPMENTS TO DIRECT SHIPMENTS (4)	INDEX OF RESOURCE TRADE (5)
24.	IRON ORES	.026	-.074	-.255	.222	.799
25.	GOLD AND PLATINUM ORES	.001	-.013	-.683	.114	1.000
26.	COAL	.040	-.074	-.050	7.776	-.893
27.	CRUDE MINERAL OILS	.060	-.190	-.305	.330	-.002
28.	NATURAL GAS	.003	-.005	-.027	.046	.592
29.	OTHER BITUMINOUS	.000	-.000	-.408	.028	.311
30.	SULPHUR	.005	-.004	.333	.195	.684
31.	ASBESTOS	.001	-.005	-.405	.018	.981
32.	GYPSUM	.000	-.000	-.362	.028	.885
33.	SALT	.002	-.002	.071	.951	-.056
34.	PEATMOSS	.000	-.000	-.051	.002	1.000
35.	CLAY AND OTHER	.002	-.004	-.077	3.004	-.738
36.	ABRASIVES	.001	-.004	-.331	R	-1.000
37.	NON-METALLIC MINERALS	.010	-.016	.034	.815	-.111
38.	SAND AND GRAVELS	.003	-.007	-.177	10.987	-.907
39.	STONE	.005	-.009	-.072	3.073	-.530

[I] BOTH RESOURCE EXPORTS AND RESOURCE IMPORTS ARE ZERO.

[R] RESOURCE EXPORTS ARE ZERO.

Canada has a surplus in Minerals and metals at the resource stage and in terms of resources traded as part of the value of commodities. This is true for the world as a whole and for every region in the world.

In trade with the world as a whole, Canada by 1969 exports energy, but the energy required to produce commodity exports is less than that required to produce the commodities imported. At the resource stage, Canada is a net exporter, but is a net importer in terms of the commodities traded. This pattern is the same in Canada's trade with all areas except for exports to the United Kingdom, as part of the value of commodities exceeds imports.

The differences in the trade patterns between regions may reflect differences in resource endowments, trade restrictions, or other cost factors which are better understood in terms of disaggregated data discussed in the following sections.

RELATIVE IMPORTANCE OF RESOURCES IN COMMODITY PRODUCTION
– DISAGGREGATED RESOURCES 1967-9

Table 5 provides a somewhat different perspective on the role of resources in Canadian trade. In column 5 of the table the index of the direction of trade (formula 1) is given. This must vary from +1 to –1. In some cases, such as Milk (5), there was no trade in either direction. In such cases, the letter I appears. The index of direction of trade in each unprocessed resource in column 5 should be compared to the index of direction of trade through the value of processed commodities as indicated in column 3. We note, for example, from column 5 of Table 5 that Live animals (1) are exported in the form of a resource but, from column 3, we determine that they are reimported as part of the value of processed commodities. Columns 1 and 2 in Table 5 indicate the relative importance of trade in resources as part of the value of commodities. The items in both column 1 and column 2 add to one. Each figure in each column is the proportion of the total resource exported (or imported) as part of the value of commodities. Of the total resource cost of all exported commodities, Live animals (1) accounted for 4.6 per cent. If Canadian imports were produced in Canada, 9.8 per cent of the cost (at 1961 prices) would be used to purchase the Live animals (1) needed for processing. The figures reported in column 4 of Table 5 report the absolute value of the ratio of net trade in each resource as part of the value of processed commodities to the net trade in the resource directly. In the case of Live animals (1), net trade in processed form as part of the value of commodities is more than twice as important (2.222) as the trade in the form of unprocessed resources. The letter R appears if there are no exports of the resource in unprocessed form.

Average trade figures were used in the calculations for Table 5, along with technical coefficients estimated from the 1961 input-output matrix as described above. The principal results from Table 5 are discussed below. Readers interested in the 1961 and 1969 data may refer to Tables 6 and 7.

The first fifteen items on the list in Table 5 are a disaggregation of what, in the previous discussion, we called Agricultural resources. Item 2, omitted from the table, is Rice (2), which is part of the aggregated classification Non-competing resources. These data indicate that Canada is not a nation with a broad agricultural base. Of the fourteen categories of Agricultural resources, Canada is a significant exporter in only six. A large number of Agricultural resources are imported, and a number of others are not produced in Canada at all (e.g. cotton, sugar cane, coffee, tea, rice, natural rubber, and some tropical fruits). Canadian agricultural exports typically exceed imports by about one-third.

Under the circumstances it is not surprising to find that Agricultural resources account for so little of the value of exported commodities. From column 1 of Table 5 the reader may verify that no Agricultural resource except Live animals (1) accounts for much over 2 per cent of the total resource cost of Canadian exports. Canadian abundance in Agricultural resources is largely attributable to exports of Wheat (3) and Oil seed and oil nuts (11). While these may establish a comparative advantage in some restricted line (e.g. flour and feed meal), they are apparently insufficient to establish a broad base for food processing. Canada also suffers the disadvantage of being located near the United States, which has a broadly based agriculture and which exports most of the Agricultural resources that are exported from Canada. Imports of Agricultural resources must pay Canadian tariffs and are otherwise restricted (and in some cases, embargoed) by non-tariff barriers. This increases costs in food processing. Also, in many lines economies of scale are involved in food processing (Eastman and Stykolt, 1967, 111-90). Given the greater range and quantity of resource supplies and the larger market, the United States tends to be a lower cost location than Canada.

The reader will recall from the discussion above that Canada exports Agricultural resources to the United Kingdom and Japan in unprocessed form, and also that more is exported to these areas as part of the value of commodities than is imported. With regard to the United States, however, both flows are reversed, and in Canada's trade with EEC there is a net import as part of the value of commodities. This would appear to provide some empirical verification of the factors discussed in the preceding paragraph. Although Canada exports more Agricultural resources than she imports, her agricultural base is too narrow to support an amount of agricultural processing for export greater than the amount imported. Canada, in fact, is a net importer of a large number of Agricultural resources, and tariff and non-tariff barriers raise the costs of these to Canadian processors. In addition, the US and EEC tariffs prevent Canada from achieving economies of scale in lines where she has an exportable surplus of resources which might otherwise be exported in processed form.

TABLE 6

Direct and indirect trade in thirty-nine resources, 1961

NO. NAME OF CLASSIFICATION	PERCENTAGE OF TOTAL RESOURCE EXPORTS (1)	INDIRECT RESOURCE IMPORTS (2)	INDEX OF TRADE THROUGH COMMODITIES (3)	RATIO: INDIRECT SHIPMENTS TO DIRECT SHIPMENTS (4)	INDEX OF RESOURCE TRADE (5)
1. LIVE ANIMALS	.053	-.106	-.025	1.136	.052
3. WHEAT	.020	-.015	.421	.049	1.339
4. OTHER GRAIN	.010	-.021	-.081	.297	.412
5. MILK	.015	-.022	.123	R	.000
6. EGGS	.001	-.003	-.116	.740	-.012
7. HONEY AND BEESWAX	.000	-.000	-.188	.317	.026
8. NUTS, FRUITS, BERRIES	.002	-.013	-.481	.354	-.587
9. VEGETABLES	.004	-.024	-.489	.650	-.358
10. HAY, GRASS AND NURSERY	.002	-.002	.175	.250	-.256
11. OIL SEED OIL NUTS	.005	-.030	-.557	.096	.318
12. HOPS	.000	-.000	.231	3.646	-1.855
13. TOBACCO	.008	-.005	.496	R	.000
14. FUR	.000	-.007	-.754	.028	.183
15. WOOL IN THE GREASE	.001	-.068	-.640	.967	-1.140
16. LOGS AND BOLTS	.117	-.052	.616	26.834	-.013
17. POLES AND PIT PROPS	.001	-.002	-.007	.236	.202
18. PULPWOOD	.180	-.057	.713	10.302	.060
19. OTHER CRUDE WOOD	.001	-.001	.024	.159	.133
20. CUSTOM FORESTRY	.036	-.014	.659	R	.000
21. FISH LANDINGS	.047	-.016	.691	4.831	.085
22. METAL ORES	.326	-.187	.532	10.883	-.057
23. RADIO-ACTIVE ORES	.037	-.021	.542	.260	.736

TABLE 6 continued

NO. NAME OF CLASSIFICATION	PERCENTAGE OF TOTAL RESOURCE EXPORTS (1)	INDIRECT RESOURCE IMPORTS (2)	INDEX OF TRADE THROUGH COMMODITIES (3)	RATIO: INDIRECT SHIPMENTS TO DIRECT SHIPMENTS (4)	INDEX OF RESOURCE TRADE (5)
24. IRON ORES	.016	-.063	-.342	.191	.443
25. GOLD AND PLATINUM ORES	.001	-.012	-.686	.010	.966
26. COAL	.032	-.065	-.036	5.523	-1.624
27. CRUDE MINERAL OILS	.054	-.196	-.316	.466	-.366
28. NATURAL GAS	.002	-.005	.003	.084	.568
29. OTHER BITUMINOUS	.000	-.000	-.068	.009	.962
30. SULPHUR	.005	-.004	.378	1.837	-.419
31. ASBESTOS	.001	-.006	-.574	.009	.959
32. GYPSUM	.000	-.000	-.487	.016	.910
33. SALT	.002	-.003	.097	1.066	.032
34. PEATMOSS	.000	-.000	-.013	.001	.981
35. CLAY	.002	-.004	-.066	1.590	-1.273
36. ABRASIVES	.001	-.004	-.308	385.648	-90.517
37. NON-METALLIC MINERALS	.009	-.016	.018	2.259	-.824
38. SAND AND GRAVELS	.002	-.007	-.204	6.768	-.175
39. STONE	.004	-.009	-.068	3.986	-.209

R DIRECT SHIPMENTS ARE ZERO.

TABLE 7

Direct and indirect trade in thirty-nine resources, 1969

NO.	NAME OF CLASSIFICATION	PERCENTAGE OF TOTAL INDIRECT		INDEX OF TRADE THROUGH COMMODITIES	RATIO: INDIRECT SHIPMENTS TO DIRECT SHIPMENTS	INDEX OF RESOURCE TRADE
		RESOURCE EXPORTS (1)	RESOURCE IMPORTS (2)	(3)	(4)	(5)
1.	LIVE ANIMALS	.047	-.106	-.175	2.373	.439
3.	WHEAT	.014	-.012	.273	.087	1.000
4.	OTHER GRAIN	.010	-.017	-.027	.903	-.149
5.	MILK	.012	-.018	.028	R	I
6.	EGGS	.001	-.002	-.138	2.377	-.747
7.	HONEY AND BEESWAX	.000	-.000	-.235	.409	.267
8.	NUTS, FRUITS, BERRIES	.002	-.010	-.454	.419	-.685
9.	VEGETABLES	.005	-.017	-.392	.653	-.758
10.	HAY, GRASS AND NURSERY	.002	-.002	.105	.293	-.245
11.	OIL SEED OIL NUTS	.005	-.022	-.449	.164	.130
12.	HOPS	.000	-.000	.334	4.039	-.794
13.	TOBACCO	.009	-.004	.502	R	I
14.	FUR	.001	-.007	-.494	.119	.122
15.	WOOL IN THE GREASE	.001	-.006	-.490	6.020	-.694
16.	LOGS AND BOLTS	.128	-.050	.605	29.473	-.397
17.	POLES AND PIT PROPS	.001	-.002	-.030	.433	.812
18.	PULPWOOD	.164	-.050	.680	20.330	.777
19.	OTHER CRUDE WOOD	.001	-.001	-.025	.354	.887
20.	CUSTOM FORESTRY	.035	-.013	.631	R	I
21.	FISH LANDINGS	.040	-.010	.731	1.912	.404
22.	METAL ORES	.316	-.223	.386	2.134	.424
23.	RADIO-ACTIVE ORES	.036	-.025	.394	3.992	1.000

TABLE 7 continued

NO.	NAME OF CLASSIFICATION	PERCENTAGE OF TOTAL RESOURCE EXPORTS (1)	INDIRECT RESOURCE IMPORTS (2)	INDEX OF TRADE THROUGH COMMODITIES (3)	RATIO: INDIRECT SHIPMENTS TO DIRECT SHIPMENTS (4)	INDEX OF RESOURCE TRADE (5)
24.	IRON ORES	.028	-.075	-.257	.297	.789
25.	GOLD AND PLATINUM ORES	.002	-.013	-.664	.137	1.000
26.	COAL	.042	-.075	-.057	12.759	-.908
27.	CRUDE MINERAL OILS	.063	-.181	-.287	.326	.043
28.	NATURAL GAS	.003	-.005	-.025	.045	.746
29.	OTHER BITUMINOUS	.000	-.000	.417	3.226	-.953
30.	SULPHUR	.005	-.004	.326	.230	.930
31.	ASBESTOS	.001	-.005	-.380	.019	.981
32.	GYPSUM	.000	-.000	-.333	.031	.898
33.	SALT	.002	-.002	.049	1.150	-.114
34.	PEATMOSS	.000	-.000	-.077	.002	1.000
35.	CLAY AND OTHER	.002	-.004	-.069	4.313	-.850
36.	ABRASIVES	.001	-.004	-.334	R	-1.000
37.	NON-METALLIC MINERALS	.010	-.016	.023	.745	.031
38.	SAND AND GRAVELS	.003	-.007	-.161	13.763	-.921
39.	STONE	.005	-.009	-.068	3.217	-.460

I BOTH RESOURCE EXPORTS AND RESOURCE IMPORTS ARE ZERO.

R RESOURCE EXPORTS ARE ZERO.

It is perhaps worth noting for reference below that the value of Live animals (1) required to produce Canadian exports and the value of the Live animals (1) that would be required to produce the commodities Canada imports constitute significant percentages of the total cost of Canada's traded commodities compared to other Agricultural resources and resources in general.

The tables based on the aggregated resource classes revealed that Canada exports Forestry resources in unprocessed form and that the value of Forestry resources required to produce Canada's commodity exports exceeds the value of Forestry resources that would be required to produce Canada's imports. This is consistent with the hypothesis that Forestry resources are a source of Canadian comparative advantage in processing. Forestry resources are an aggregation of resources 16 to 20 in Table 5. It appears that Pulpwood (18), Logs and bolts (16), and Custom forestry (20) accounted for nearly one-third of the value of Canada's exports of processed commodities. The ratio of the value of net Forestry resources exported through the value of commodities to net exports of unprocessed resources is higher in the case of Logs and bolts (16) and Pulpwood (18) than in any other resource category. It would appear that Forestry resources are an important source of cost advantage to Canadian producers, yet, interestingly, Canada imported almost 30 per cent of her Logs and bolts (16) in 1961.

Items 22 through 25 and 30 through 39 in Table 5 are part of the resource classification Minerals and metals, which according to Table 2 are exported as resources and as part of the value of commodities. This classification is dominated by Metal ores (22), which are also exported as resources and as part of the value of commodities. The metals (22 to 25) account for 40 per cent of the value of Canadian commodity exports. Metal ores (22) alone accounted for 33 per cent of the value of Canadian commodity exports in the period 1967 to 1969. Metal ores (22) also accounted for a large percentage of the value (22 per cent) of the commodities which Canada imports but the net effect is a substantial export both in unprocessed form and as part of the value of commodities.

Iron ores (24) and Gold and platinum ores (25) are exported as unprocessed resources but not through trade in commodities. Canada also exports a substantial value of Asbestos (31) and Gypsum (32) but imports these as part of the value of commodities.

Items 26 to 29 are Energy resources. In commodity trade, Coal (26) and Crude mineral oils (27) are the two categories of greatest significance. The two together account for over one-fourth of the import displacements of resources through commodity trade and both were also imported directly.

In general, one may conclude from inspection of columns 1 and 2 of Table 5 that the total cost of the resources required to produce exports were dominated by the costs of Metal ores (22), Pulpwood (18), and Logs and bolts (16), while the total cost of commodities imported into Canada were dominated by the cost of Crude mineral oils (27), Live animals (1), Iron ores (24), and Coal (26) and Metal ores (22).

DETAILED RESOURCE TRADE WITH VARIOUS REGIONS

Tables similar to Table 5 are prepared for Canada's trade with the United States, the EEC, EFTA, Japan and the United Kingdom. These data appear as Tables A3, A4, A5, A6, and A7 in the appendix. The patterns of direct trade in resources and the characteristics of the resource costs of commodities traded are similar in each region to the world as a whole. As one would expect, trade with the world as a whole is most similar to trade with the United States. The value of Pulpwood (18) and Logs and bolts (16) required to produce commodities traded with the United States are nearly the same as the world as a whole, but the value of Metal ores (22) is somewhat less. Exports of Metal ores (22) dominate Canada's commodity trade with all regions and in the case of the United Kingdom are 48 per cent of the cost of exports. The pattern of the resource value in commodity imports is less variant from region to region than the patterns of resource value in commodity exports. The most notable differences in the trade patterns among the regions are listed below.

The value of the Wheat (3) required to produce Canadian commodity exports to the world is greater than the value of the Wheat (3) which would be required for Canada to produce her own commodity imports, but the value of Wheat (3) in Canada's commodity trade with the EEC and EFTA constitutes an import displacement. The importation of Wheat (3) in processed form as part of the value of commodities would appear to run counter to the ideal of world specialization.

Similarly, Canadian commodity exports require more Tobacco (13) than her imports, but this is reversed in Canada's trade with the United States.

Although Canada exports Other grain (4) to the world as a whole, the value of Other grain (4) required to produce Canada's commodity imports exceeds the cost of Other grain (4) required to produce her exports. In trade with the United States, the United Kingdom and Japan, this is reversed. Also, the value of Milk (5) and Tobacco (13) required to produce Canada's commodity exports exceed the cost of Milk (5) and Tobacco (13) that would be required to produce commodity imports. The export of Milk (5) in processed form is due entirely to trade with Japan and the United Kingdom. Canada imports tobacco in processed form from the EEC and the United States.

Trade in Agricultural resources with the United Kingdom tends most frequently to run in a counter direction to the trade flow with the rest of the world. Hops (12) are normally exported as part of the value of commodities but are imported in this form from the United Kingdom. Of the Agricultural resources normally imported, Live animals (1), Other grain (4), Eggs (6), Honey and beeswax (7), Nuts, fruits and berries (8), Vegetables (9), and Oil seed and oil nuts (11) are exported as part of the value of processed commodities.

Unlike her direct resource trade with the world as a whole, Canada has an export surplus of Vegetables (9) and Hay, grass and nursery (10) to Japan.

It is generally believed that Canada does not have a comparative advantage in Milk (5) production.[3] Nevertheless, the value of Milk (5) required to produce commodities exported exceeds the cost of Milk (5) required to produce imports. The net export of Milk (5) through commodity trade does not hold in trade with the United States, the EEC, or EFTA but is apparently achieved in trade with the United Kingdom and Japan.

The pattern of trade in Forestry resources in unprocessed form and the characteristics of trade in commodities which holds for the world as a whole also holds with a minor exception for each region. Canada exports unprocessed Forestry resources, and the value of Forestry resources required to produce Canadian exports exceeds the value that would be required to produce her imports. Logs and bolts (16) are imported from the United States but are exported in resource form to all other regions. Other crude wood (19) is imported from Japan but exported to the world as a whole. In trade with the United Kingdom, both Poles and pit props (17) and Other crude wood (19) are a net export through the value of commodities, but are a net import from the world as a whole.

The import-export relationship with regard to Metal ores (22) which holds for the world as a whole also holds for every region whether we look at unprocessed trade flows or at the value of metals shipped as part of the value of processed commodities.

Regional trade in Energy resources has a pattern governed by transport costs. Coal (26) is exported from Eastern Canada to the EEC and from Western Canada to Japan, although in terms of total trade Canada imports Coal (26). All energy resources are a net import as part of the cost of commodities, except Other bituminous (29), which is exported. This holds in the United States and EEC trade, but Canada exports Crude mineral oils (27) to Japan and imports Other bituminous (29) through commodity trade. All energy resources are a net export

3 This we may judge from the amount of subsidy and the embargo on importation of milk products (see Report of the Federal Task Force on Agriculture (1969)).

to the United Kingdom through commodity trade, including Other bituminous (29), which is also imported through commodity trade from EFTA.

The direction of trade in unprocessed mineral resources in certain cases is in the reverse direction to Canada's trade with the world as a whole. Gypsum (32) is imported from the EEC and from the United Kingdom but exported to the rest of the world. Non-metallic minerals (37) are exported to the EEC but imported from the rest of the world. Salt (33) is exported to the United States but imported from all other areas. When we calculate the cost of minerals required to produce commodity imports and exports, the pattern is similar to the world as a whole with minor exceptions. The cost of Salt (33) from the EEC and EFTA required to produce imports is greater than the cost of Salt (33) required to produce exports.

These regional differences are explained in part by the differences in transport costs between Canada and other regions and within Canada. As noted above, Western coal is more economically shipped to Japan than to Ontario, which purchases coal from the United States. Also, regions differ in their resource endowments compared to Canada and to each other. In so far as commodity trade is determined by resource endowments, one expects to find differences in Canada's commodity trade by region. The resource requirements of commodities are the subject of the following section.

RESOURCE REQUIREMENTS OF COMMODITIES

General aspects of Table A2 have already received commentary. This table also has a more explicit use. The resource use of commodities can be identified at a disaggregated level. The reader will recall the general features of this table. The first column of Table A2 shows the net trade of each commodity (exports less imports) expressed as a percentage of output for the year 1961 for the commodity classifications indicated. The remaining columns report on the resource use of each commodity. The amount of each resource used by each commodity is expressed as a percentage of total Canadian productive use. The table therefore describes the manner in which resources disappear as they are used to produce commodities. The general classes of resources used above are aggregations of the resources depicted in Table A2. Columns numbered 1 to 15 are concerned with Agricultural resources, columns 16 to 20 are with Forestry resources, column 21 is reserved for Fish landings (21), columns 22 to 25 report on the use of Metals, columns 26 to 29 report on Energy, and columns 30 to 39 are concerned with Minerals. On the basis of these more detailed data, let us reconsider the conclusions of the previous sections.

Our general results in the first section established that Canada's trade in commodities could be regarded as an exchange of Canadian exports of natural resources for imports of labour and capital and that the exchange of resources, labour, and capital through commodities was of increasing significance relative to the direct flow in international trade of unprocessed resources. If this holds also for particular resources, we would expect to discover that, in cases where Canada was exporting more of an unprocessed resource than it imported, this would also be reflected increasingly in her commodity trade. An implicit hypothesis is present which asserts that Canada's comparative advantage at the resource stage should establish a comparative advantage in processing. Under this hypothesis there is particular interest in lowering foreign tariff barriers against Canadian processed goods if such goods use resources which are more abundant in Canada than outside Canada. Such growth of Canadian industry is more likely to be a change in the direction of the Canadian comparative advantage.

It was noted in the previous sections that there has been a net import replacement of Agricultural resources through trade in processed commodities, even though Canada is a net exporter of unprocessed Agricultural resources. Furthermore, compared to exports, a greater percentage of Canadian agricultural imports come in as part of the value of commodities than in unprocessed form. Finally, we determined that trade as part of the cost of processed commodities is growing relative to trade in unprocessed resources. How can Canada increase the level of processing of Agricultural resources without further increasing restrictions on imports?

The answer was given, at least in part, in the previous sections. The fact that Canada is a net importer of Agricultural resources as part of the cost of processed commodities is due largely to Canada's trade with the United States. Canada has succeeded in exporting Agricultural resources as part of the cost of processed commodities to the United Kingdom and Japan, and apparently these areas represent opportunities for expansion of processed agriculture. We also noted that Canada's net export of Agricultural resources is a consequence of a large volume export of a few resource classes and that many Agricultural resources are imported.

In 1961 and in 1969, Canada had a substantial export surplus of Live animals (1), Wheat (3), Honey and beeswax (7), and Oil seeds and nuts (11). Table A2 shows that Wheat (3) and Oil seeds and nuts (11) are resources used principally by particular commodities – Feed meal and flour (50), Wheat flour, malt and starch (51), and Processed foods (49). Of these, Feed meal and flour (50) and Wheat flour, malt and starch (51) were exported from Canada in the sixties over foreign tariffs and despite transport costs. These apparently represent channels of commodity trade through which Canada can export Agricultural resources which are relatively abundant.

The Food processing (49) industry was responsible in 1961 for using 6 per cent of the Wheat (3), 16 per cent of the Other grains (4), and nearly 80 per cent of the Oil seeds and nuts (11) processed in Canada. These are all resources which were exported in unprocessed form in 1961. Specific commodities within the Food processing (49) classification which use these resources in greatest proportion should have better prospects than commodities processed from Rice (2) or those items in the classifications Nuts, fruits and berries (8) and Vegetables (9) which are imported.

Canada exports Forestry resources in unprocessed form, while there is also a net export through international commodity trade. Of the value of Logs and bolts (16) which enter into further processing in Canada, 87 per cent is used in the production of Wood products (70). This classification includes production of lumber, timber, railway ties, shingles, veneer, and plywood (see Table A1). Similarly, we find that three-fourths of the Pulpwood (18) produced in Canada is a resource used to produce Pulp and paper products (73). This classification is responsible for Canadian production of newsprint.

The discussion and tables in the preceding sections established the importance of Minerals and metals in Canadian commodity trade. Canada is a net exporter of Minerals and metals in unprocessed form to every region considered, and the cost of the Minerals and metals required to produce Canadian exports exceeds the amount of import displacement through commodity trade. Four exported ores accounted for Canada's exports of Minerals and metals in the period 1967-9. These are Metal ores (22), Radioactive ores (23), Iron ores (24), and Gold and platinum ores (25). Approximately 88 per cent of the Metal ores (22) and Radioactive ores (23) used in Canadian processing are used to produce Non-ferrous metal products (81) and (83). These are products at the early stages of processing and include primary forms and alloys made from nickel, copper, lead, tin, and zinc and later stages in which there is casting, rolling, extruding, or fabricating.

Although Canada exports Iron ores (24) in unprocessed form, the cost of the Iron ores (24) used to produce exports is less than that which would be required to produce commodity imports. In Canada, Iron ores (24) are processed into commodities by the import-competing classification Iron and steel intermediate (79), which meets fairly heavy import competition, and (77), which operates in the domestic market in isolation from import competition. The group of producers which has most successfully penetrated foreign markets is the export classification (80), but these producers in 1961 used only 11 per cent of the Iron ores (24) processed in Canada.

Gold and platinum ores (25) are used to produce a variety of products, but Canada is a substantial importer of these through her commodity trade. Of the amount of Gold and platinum ores (25) processed in Canada, 59 per cent are used to produce Jewelry (106).

There is no discernible relationship between Canada's mineral resources and its commodity trade. Large percentages of Asbestos (31) are exported in unprocessed form. The principal user classification is Mineral products (94), which also uses 41 per cent of domestic consumption of Gypsum (32), which is also an exported Mineral resource. Mineral products (94) is an import-competing classification producing a variety of products, including plasters, porcelain insulators and fittings, vitreous china and houseware of china and porcelain, refractories, products of stone and clay, mineral wool, thermal insulation, asbestos-cement products, and products made from glass. Mineral products (94) is a substantial user of Gypsum (32), but classification (93) is the principal user, taking 51 per cent of the supplies used in Canadian processing. The output consists of heavier products, such as cement, lime, concrete, bricks, and abrasives produced primarily for the local market.

RESOURCES AND THE DEGREE OF PROCESSING

Our objective in this study is to clarify the relationship between resources, as they affect comparative advantage through resource cost, and tariffs, as they affect production by altering relative prices. As noted in the first chapter, the comparative advantage generated by Canada's resource base is not actually observable in equilibrium cost comparisons because unit costs tend to be equalized through trade. On the other hand, tariffs have the purpose and effect of maintaining observable cost differences among nations. It is therefore very difficult to determine how these two forces may interact.

In an earlier study this author adopted a simulation approach in order to study the simultaneous impact of tariffs and resources (Williams, forthcoming). The logical approach adopted is too complex to describe completely in this place. The reader must accept a rather brief account. In the simulation, the 1961 resource usage rates were assumed to be fixed, all tariffs were set at zero, and it was assumed that all trade barriers were eliminated. With the change in relative prices which ensued, there would be changes in costs and prices in each commodity classification. Each commodity lost direct tariff protection, but offsetting this there was a reduction in cost. Intermediate goods would be available at international prices free of Canadian duty, and Canadian prices of intermediate goods competitive with imports would also be lower. The results of the simulation are reported in Table 8.

There are two groups of commodities listed in Table 8. The expanding group represents those commodity classifications which would be most favoured by the relative price changes following free trade. The contracting group are those which would be affected unfavourably. The reader should understand that the results apply to the cost structure of the classifications considered and will not apply to individual cases of commodities with cost structures different from the average for the group.

TABLE 8

Effects of relative price changes under free trade, 1961

Classification	Ratio: Intermediate shipments / Total supply
Expanding	
56 Liquor and beer	0.09
57 Alcohol and wine	0.19
59 Rubber products	0.40
61 Rubber products	0.91
63 Textile products, cotton	0.90
76 Printing	0.63
82 Non-ferrous metal products	0.93
87 Aircraft incl., parts	0.99
88 Autos, trucks and parts	0.41
89 Buses and locomotives	0.85
90 Transportation equipment	0.30
91 Electrical appliances	0.63
102 Inorganic chemicals	0.85
105 Scientific equipment	0.90
107 Plastic products	0.81
109 End products	0.61
Contracting	
49 Processed foods	0.35
54 Beet, pulp and sugar	0.56
62 Leather goods	0.08
66 Textiles, silk and synth.	0.92
67 Textile products NES	0.22
68 Textile products NES	0.28
69 Fur	0.01
78 Graphite and carbon	1.00
80 Iron and steel intermediate	1.00
85 Agricultural machinery	0.97
86 Other machinery and equipment	0.92
100 Pharmaceuticals	0.37
104 Industrial chemicals	0.91

The classifications designated as expanding in Table 8 are those which, considering Canada's 1961 resource usage rate, operated at relatively too low a level. Since most of these are import-competing, foreign tariffs have little impact, and removal of foreign tariffs would not be expected to have the desired effect of expanding output. If Canada should adopt a tariff policy directed toward expansion, it would have to be achieved by reducing the cost of intermediate goods through reductions in Canadian tariff. The classifications designated as contracting were overexpanded under the 1961 tariff, compared with a situation of optimal resource use. By reducing present levels of protection in these groups, Canada would bring them to a level consistent with efficient resource use and with international prices.

THE GENERAL QUESTION OF PROCESSING

There are a number of alternatives to the simplistic definition of degree of processing thus far adopted. One is to define the degree of processing as the ratio of intermediate product shipments to total supply; this magnitude appears in column 5 of Table 9. A second definition, relevant for certain purposes, is based on the value of intermediate goods purchased per dollar of output. In this definition, end-product producers are those which purchase in greatest amount from other producers. A somewhat more general definition of the same type would take both direct and indirect purchases of intermediate goods into account. With such a definition one would include, for example, the steel required to produce an automobile, even if the automobile industry made no direct purchases of steel.

Both computations are displayed in Table 9. The items appearing in column 4 are the amounts of intermediate goods directly purchased in a given classification in order to produce one dollar's worth of output for final demand. (Final demand represents shipments to households, to government, to business firms for future use, and exports. It excludes shipments to business firms for use in production as intermediate goods in the current period). Column 8 is the direct plus indirect purchase of intermediate goods. It represents the amounts of intermediate goods required per dollar of output if all firms produced the intermediate goods they needed in their own factories rather than purchasing them from other firms.

To illustrate the distinction, consider the case of Cereal products (52). If output of Cereal products (52) should increase by one dollar, output in other firms would increase by $1.43 to produce the intermediate goods required directly and indirectly. This does not imply that income of $2.43 has been earned in the economy. When output increases by one dollar it can create no more than one dollar of value added. The figure $1.43 in column 8 indicates the amount that output (not income) is increased outside the Cereal products (52) classification. Thus, output including Cereal products (52) increases by $2.43. Value added or income in each classification is less than the value of output and must increase by the amount that final demand has increased, which equals one dollar by assumption.

The computation shown in column 8 of Table 9 indicates the extent to which it is possible to vary independently the output in any particular classification. If, for example, we are able, through tariff policy, to expand output of Cereal products (52) by one dollar, there will be an unintended expansion elsewhere of $1.43. The policy objective is, at most, 41 per cent achieved ($1/2.43 \cong 0.41$).

A similar distinction is made with regard to resource purchases. Column 3 in Table 9 is the amount per dollar spent directly on resources by the firms in the classification considered. This must be less than the value shown in column 6, which shows the direct plus indirect resource use. A firm producing automobiles, for example, might purchase little or no Iron ores (24) directly, and column 3 would be zero. If we take account of purchases of intermediate goods in automobile production, however, we would expect to find that there is significant content of Iron ores (24) in automobiles, and this would appear as part of direct plus indirect purchase of domestic resources in column 6. Similarly, column 7 indicates direct plus indirect use of imported resources. The greater the amount of domestic resource required, the more a commodity classification is benefiting from the Canadian resource endowment. On the other hand, dependence on foreign resources usually implies a higher cost of producers located in Canada and a comparative disadvantage on that account.

A distinction has been made in Table 9 between the direction and magnitude of trade. The magnitude of trade is the ratio of the sum of exports plus imports over output. The direction of trade is the ratio of exports less imports over exports plus imports. The magnitude of trade is the best indicator of the significance of the trade sector in each commodity group. The direction index is needed because some classifications are more heterogeneous than others, so that trade in one direction may offset trade in the other direction. Alternatively, this may arise because of transport costs, even in homogeneous classifications. To return to our example above, coal is exported from both Eastern Canada and Western Canada, but imported into Ontario. If the magnitude of trade is large and if the index of direction is large and positive, foreign tariffs have the greatest influence on trade, and in such cases the Canadian tariff becomes redundant. If the magnitude of trade is large and if the index of direction is negative and numerically large, the Canadian tariff has the predominant influence on trade and foreign tariffs may be redundant. If the magnitude of trade is near zero, it is not possible to determine which tariff has the predominant influence.

The data of Table 9 may be used for consideration of certain non-economic objectives. Since there are too many classifications for us to consider all aspects of these data, we confine our attention to an illustration. Suppose it is desired that output of Fur (69) should be expanded. It might be argued that Fur (69) is an end-product producer because the index (column 5) is 0.01. In the sense

TABLE 9

Trade indices, fraction of costs spent on resources and intermediate goods per dollar of output, and intermediate shipments per dollar of output

CLASSIFICATION NO. VERBAL NAME	TRADE INDICES		FRACTION OF COST SPENT ON:			DIRECT PLUS INDIRECT PURCHASES OF		
	MAGNITUDE (1)	DIRECTION (2)	RESOURCES (3)	INTERMEDIATE GOODS (4)	INTERMEDIATE SHIPMENTS (5)	DOMESTIC RESOURCES (6)	NON-COMPETING RESOURCES (7)	OTHER GOODS (8)
40. SERVICES TO AGRICULTURE	.00	.00	.04	.42	.95	.16	.00	.98
41. SERVICES TO MINING	.00	.00	.01	.43	1.00	.07	.00	1.00
42. MEAT	.28	-.04	.45	.76	.27	.64	.00	1.65
43. MARGARINE AND SHORTENING	.11	.05	.36	.80	.43	.53	.05	1.76
44. HIDES AND SKINS	1.05	.13	.42	.73	1.00	.60	.01	1.60
45. CRUDE ANIMAL PRODUCTS	.22	.28	.52	.85	.97	.73	.01	1.86
46. POULTRY PROCESSED	.03	-.96	.36	.68	.23	.52	.00	1.47
47. DAIRY PRODUCTS	.04	.34	.55	.79	.22	.71	.01	1.67
48. FISH PRODUCTS	.79	.73	.49	.78	.43	.60	.00	1.51
49. PROCESSED FOODS	.31	-.76	.16	.69	.35	.28	.07	1.55
50. FEED MEAL AND FLOUR	.03	.34	.30	.87	.96	.52	.02	2.05
51. WHEAT FLOUR, MALT STARCH	.15	.98	.28	.73	.41	.42	.03	1.63
52. CEREAL PRODUCTS	.96	-.54	.03	.60	.13	.17	.03	1.43
53. CONFECTIONARY PRODUCTS	.07	-.77	.05	.67	.01	.17	.11	1.48
54. BEET, PULP AND SUGAR	.25	.99	.07	.60	.56	.18	.11	1.29
55. SUGAR REFINERY PRODUCTS	.05	-.75	.11	.71	.57	.15	.44	1.03
56. LIQUOR AND BEER	.34	.27	.04	.51	.09	.13	.00	1.20
57. ALCOHOL AND WINE	.55	-.79	.14	.56	.19	.22	.04	1.20
58. TOBACCO, PROCESSED	.11	.51	.31	.77	.25	.51	.00	1.80
59. RUBBER PRODUCTS	.11	-.78	.01	.57	.40	.07	.09	1.22
60. LEATHER	.35	.11	.01	.74	1.00	.30	.01	1.79
61. RUBBER PRODUCTS	.29	-.79	.01	.56	.91	.08	.07	1.21
62. LEATHER GOODS	.16	-.77	.00	.60	.08	.11	.01	1.48
63. TEXTILE PRODUCTS, COTTON	.66	-.85	.00	.65	.90	.06	.22	1.26

TABLE 9 continued

CLASSIFICATION NO. VERBAL NAME	TRADE INDICES		FRACTION OF COST SPENT ON			DIRECT PLUS INDIRECT PURCHASES OF		
	MAGNITUDE (1)	DIRECTION (2)	RESOURCES (3)	INTERMEDIATE GOODS (4)	INTERMEDIATE SHIPMENTS (5)	DOMESTIC RESOURCES (6)	NON-COMPETING RESOURCES (7)	OTHER GOODS (8)
64. YARN OF WOOL HAIR	.24	-.91	.02	.64	.61	.10	.04	1.46
65. TEXTILE PRODUCTS,WOOL	.74	-.86	.06	.61	.91	.14	.04	1.40
66. TEXTILES SILK AND SYNT.	.34	-.52	.00	.58	.92	.09	.02	1.32
67. TEXTILE PRODUCTS N.E.S.,M	.17	-.89	.02	.63	.22	.08	.04	1.44
68. TEXTILE PRODUCTS N.E.S.,M	.25	-.83	.01	.61	.28	.08	.03	1.40
69. FUR	.02	-.20	.03	.63	.01	.09	.04	1.42
70. WOOD PRODUCTS,E	.56	.74	.37	.63	1.00	.51	.00	1.38
71. WOOD PRODUCTS,M	.12	-.20	.14	.60	.95	.29	.00	1.34
72. WOOD PRODUCTS,M	.12	-.26	.03	.58	.42	.16	.01	1.34
73. PULP AND PAPER PRODUCTS,E	.86	.98	.23	.53	.99	.37	.00	1.14
74. PULP AND PAPER PRODUCTS,M	.27	-.39	.18	.56	.90	.32	.00	1.23
75. PULP AND PAPER PRODUCTS,M	.11	-.50	.08	.62	.91	.22	.00	1.42
76. PRINTING	.24	-.90	.00	.45	.63	.09	.00	1.00
77. IRON AND STEEL INTERMED	.29	-.62	.07	.58	1.00	.19	.00	1.31
78. GRAPHITE AND CARBON	.44	-.79	.21	.61	1.00	.36	.00	1.29
79. IRON AND STEEL INTERMED,M	.11	-.09	.09	.57	1.00	.21	.00	1.28
80. IRON AND STEEL INTERMED,E	.53	.93	.20	.56	1.00	.33	.00	1.22
81. NONFERROUS METAL PROD.,E	.61	.87	.42	.80	.99	.66	.00	1.52
82. NONFERROUS METAL PROD.,M	.33	-.56	.00	.61	.93	.17	.00	1.44
83. NONFERROUS METAL PROD.,E	.61	.09	.16	.71	.92	.40	.00	1.55
84. PLUMBING MISC.EQUIP.	.53	-.86	.00	.58	.97	.12	.00	1.35
85. AGRICULTURAL MACHINERY	2.08	-.44	.00	.60	.97	.09	.00	1.37
86. OTHER MACHINERY AND EQUIP.	1.09	-.79	.01	.53	.92	.10	.00	1.19
87. AIRCRAFT INC. PARTS	.80	-.29	.00	.52	.99	.07	.00	1.19

TABLE 9 continued

CLASSIFICATION NO. VERBAL NAME	TRADE INDICES		FRACTION OF COST SPENT ON			DIRECT PLUS INDIRECT PURCHASES OF		
	MAGNITUDE (1)	DIRECTION (2)	RESOURCES (3)	INTERMEDIATE GOODS (4)	INTERMEDIATE SHIPMENTS (5)	DOMESTIC RESOURCES (6)	NON-COMPETING RESOURCES (7)	OTHER GOODS (8)
88. AUTOS, TRUCKS AND PARTS	.51	-.87	.00	.69	.41	.08	.01	1.73
89. BUSES AND LOCOMOTIVES	.46	-.52	.00	.64	.85	.10	.00	1.54
90. TRANSPORTATION EQUIPMENT	.27	-.46	.00	.46	.30	.08	.00	1.03
91. ELECTRICAL APPLIANCES	.47	-.79	.00	.55	.63	.09	.00	1.27
92. ELECTRICAL EQUIPMENT	.23	-.16	.00	.61	.60	.17	.00	1.44
93. MINERAL PRODUCTS,E	.14	.14	.09	.56	1.00	.20	.00	1.27
94. MINERAL PRODUCTS,M	.51	-.88	.06	.51	.87	.15	.00	1.15
95. PETROLEUM PRODUCTS,M	.30	-.77	.51	.75	.88	.57	.00	1.33
96. PETROLSUM PRODUCTS,M	.11	-.89	.59	.79	.58	.65	.00	1.40
97. NAPHTHA AND ASPHALT	.13	-.74	.57	.79	.96	.63	.00	1.40
98. COAL PRODUCTS N.E.S.	.61	-.66	.12	.52	.96	.23	.00	1.13
99. EXPLOSIVES	.15	-.13	.01	.52	.90	.11	.00	1.19
100. PHARMACEUTICALS	.20	-.68	.01	.62	.37	.10	.01	1.48
101. CHEMICALS	.39	.48	.06	.58	.99	.22	.00	1.29
102. INORGANIC CHEMICALS,Y	.46	-.57	.04	.61	.85	.17	.01	1.41
103. INORGANIC CHEMICALS,E	.36	.07	.06	.52	.88	.21	.00	1.13
104. INDUSTRIAL CHEMICALS	.69	-.21	.03	.54	.91	.16	.01	1.21
105. SCIENTIFIC EQUIPMENT	1.14	-.75	.00	.50	.90	.09	.00	1.17
106. JEWELRY	1.16	-.86	.07	.52	.22	.18	.00	1.19
107. PLASTICS PRODUCTS	.49	-.77	.02	.62	.81	.13	.01	1.45
108. END PRODUCTS N.E.S.,M	.44	-.80	.00	.54	.39	.09	.61	1.28
109. END PRODUCTS N.E.S.,M	.72	-.66	.03	.53	.61	.12	.00	1.23
110. DRESSING AND DYEING	.00	.00	.01	.43	1.00	.08	.00	1.00
111. CONSTRUCTION	.00	.00	.01	.58	.99	.12	.00	1.29

TABLE 9 continued

CLASSIFICATION	TRADE INDICES		FRACTION OF COST SPENT ON:			DIRECT PLUS INDIRECT PURCHASES OF		
NO. VERBAL NAME	MAGNITUDE (1)	DIRECTION (2)	RESOURCES (3)	INTERMEDIATE GOODS (4)	INTERMEDIATE SHIPMENTS (5)	DOMESTIC RESOURCES (6)	NON-COMPETING RESOURCES (7)	OTHER GOODS (8)
112. TRANSPORTATION-TRADE	.04	.64	.02	.34	.50	.08	.00	.72
113. ELECTRIC POWER	.01	.83	.01	.33	.63	.29	.00	.57
114. WATER SERVICES	.91	-.08	.03	.46	.15	.11	.00	.95
115. COMMUNICATIONS	.94	.17	.00	.22	.60	.02	.00	.43
116. BUSINESS SERVICE	.02	-.57	.01	.27	.34	.05	.00	.59
117. PERSONAL SERVICE	.07	-.90	.00	.36	.25	.04	.00	.76
118. ADVERTISING,TRAVEL	.01	-.10	.00	.87	1.00	.08	.00	1.70
119. REPAIR, SUPPLIES, SERVICE	.09	1.02	.00	.98	.89	.10	.01	1.89

defined above, such a project would be only 41 per cent effective (from column 8, $1.00/2.42 \cong 0.41$). It would require, directly and indirectly, nine cents worth of Canadian resources and four cents of foreign resources. Since 63 cents of every dollar of costs is used to purchase intermediate goods (column 4), the policy might be achieved by reducing tariffs on intermediate goods. An increase in direct tariff protection would not likely succeed. Although Canada is a net importer of Fur (69) (see column 2), the percentage of trade in Fur (69) is quite small, being equal to about 2 per cent (column 1).

3
Tariffs of Canada, the United States, Japan, and the EEC

It is the objective of this chapter to relate the magnitudes considered in chapter 2 to the levels of tariff in regions of the world which are Canada's principal trading partners. It has therefore been necessary to calculate *ad valorem* tariffs for these regions. Our task was simplified by the decision of the United Kingdom to join the Common Market. With the UK coming under the EEC tariff, it was sufficient to compute equivalent *ad valorem* tariffs for Canada, the United States, the EEC, and Japan.

Ad Valorem TARIFFS

Tariff levels in Canada, the United States, Japan and the EEC are displayed in Table 10 for commodity classifications 1 to 109. Tariffs were computed as average *ad valorem* rates at a four-digit Brussels Tariff Nomenclature level, taking the ratio of duty paid to total imports. Rates of tariffs presented in Table 10 are weighted averages of these, using Canadian 1961 output levels as weights. In certain cases, European tariff rates are variable, depending on internal variables. In such cases a proper weighted average tariff could not be computed, and a star appears in Table 10 to indicate that the tariff omits these BTN groups. In order to aid the reader in making comparisons, we have computed the difference between the Canadian and foreign tariff levels. These are displayed in columns 5, 6, and 7 of Table 10. Table 10 should be studied in conjunction with Table 9, giving the direction and magnitude of trade.

In considering the tariffs computed in Table 10, the reader should bear in mind that in many cases non-tariff barriers are more significant than tariffs in

TABLE 10

Equivalent ad valorem tariffs, Canada, US, Japan, and EEC, 1970

CLASSIFICATION	TARIFF IN				CANADIAN TARIFF LESS TARIFF IN		
NO. VERBAL NAME	CANADA	U.S.	JAPAN	E.E.C.	U.S.	JAPAN	E.E.C.
1. LIVE ANIMALS	2.7	3.9	1.4	1.3*	-1.2	1.3	1.4
2. RICE	0.0	0.0	0.0	0.0*	0.0	0.0	0.0
3. WHEAT	2.5	5.5	11.8	0.0*	-3.0	-9.3	2.5
4. OTHER GRAIN	2.6	6.7	10.7	0.0*	-4.2	-8.1	2.6
5. MILK	14.8	17.3	16.3	0.0*	-2.6	-1.5	14.8
6. EGGS	18.9	13.8	19.0	0.0*	5.1	-.1	18.9
7. HONEY AND BEESWAX	4.7	5.3	22.5	14.8	-.6	-17.8	-10.1
8. NUTS, FRUITS, BERRIES	2.9	7.2	14.6	13.4	-4.4	-11.8	-10.5
9. VEGETABLES	7.6	13.6	6.9	0.0*	-6.0	.8	7.6
10. HAY, GRASS AND NURSERY	5.2	4.4	3.6	8.6	.9	1.6	-3.4
11. OIL SEED OIL NUTS	2.0	7.3	1.9	0.0	-5.2	.1	2.0
12. HOPS	0.0	5.6	5.0	9.0	-5.6	-5.0	-9.0
13. TOBACCO	18.0	63.7	355.0	19.6	-45.7	-337.0	-1.6
14. FUR	.1	11.3	7.0	.1	-11.2	-6.9	-.1
15. WOOL IN THE GREASE	0.0	21.3	0.0	0.0	-21.3	0.0	0.0
16. LOGS AND BOLTS	2.9	0.0	.5	.8	2.9	2.5	2.2
17. POLES AND PIT PROPS	5.8	0.0	.3	1.5	5.8	5.5	4.3
18. PULPWOOD	5.8	0.0	.3	1.5	5.8	5.5	4.3
19. OTHER CRUDE WOOD	1.2	1.5	1.1	2.4	-.4	.1	-1.2
20. CUSTOM FORESTRY	0.0	0.0	0.0	0.0	0.0	0.0	0.0

NOTE: Some items in these classes are excluded because the duties are variable.

TABLE 10 continued

CLASSIFICATION		TARIFF IN				CANADIAN TARIFF LESS TARIFF IN		
NO.	VERBAL NAME	CANADA	U.S.	JAPAN	E.E.C.	U.S.	JAPAN	E.E.C.
21.	FISH LANDINGS	2.5	2.8	5.1	8.5	-.3	-2.6	-6.0
22.	METAL ORES	3.1	6.6	3.9	2.1	-3.5	-.8	.9
23.	RADIO-ACTIVE ORES	3.5	6.3	3.9	2.4	-2.8	-.4	1.1
24.	IRON ORES	1.9	1.7	.2	0.0	.2	1.8	1.9
25.	GOLD AND PLATINUM ORES	.1	13.2	.1	3.3	-13.1	-.0	-3.3
26.	COAL	0.0	0.0	.6	1.5	0.0	-.6	-1.5
27.	CRUDE MINERAL OILS	5.0	3.8	12.0	3.1	1.2	-7.0	1.9
28.	NATURAL GAS	8.7	2.1	15.1	1.5	6.6	-6.4	7.2
29.	OTHER BITUMINOUS	7.5	4.0	11.4	4.6	3.5	-3.9	2.9
30.	SULPHUR	0.0	0.0	10.0	2.0	0.0	-10.0	-2.0
31.	ASBESTOS	0.0	0.0	0.0	0.0	0.0	0.0	0.0
32.	GYPSUM	3.0	46.9	3.3	0.0	-43.9	-.3	3.0
33.	SALT	3.0	4.8	3.8	7.4	-1.8	-.8	-4.4
34.	PEATMOSS	4.2	4.4	5.2	3.0	-.2	-1.1	1.2
35.	CLAY AND OTHER	6.0	6.7	.1	.4	-.7	5.9	5.6
36.	ABRASIVES	.9	3.3	1.8	.8	-2.4	-.9	.1
37.	NON-METALLIC MINERALS	3.5	2.6	2.5	.8	.9	1.1	2.7
38.	SAND AND GRAVELS	2.9	2.1	0.0	0.0	.9	2.9	2.9

TABLE 10 continued

CLASSIFICATION	TARIFF IN				CANADIAN TARIFF LESS TARIFF IN		
NO. VERBAL NAME	CANADA	U.S.	JAPAN	E.E.C.	U.S.	JAPAN	E.E.C.
39. STONE	2.8	3.5	.4	.7	-.7	2.4	2.1
40. SERVICES TO AGRICULTURE	0.0	0.0	0.0	0.0	0.0	0.0	0.0
41. SERVICES TO MINING	0.0	0.0	0.0	0.0	0.0	0.0	0.0
42. MEAT	3.6	5.9	11.6	3.8*	-2.3	-7.9	-.2
43. MARGARINE AND SHORTENING	12.5	15.1	19.8	19.0	-2.6	-7.3	-6.6
44. HIDES AND SKINS	0.0	8.0	0.0	0.0	-8.0	0.0	0.0
45. CRUDE ANIMAL PRODUCTS	6.1	4.6	3.6	3.8	1.5	2.5	2.3
46. POULTRY PROCESSED	4.0	12.4	11.3	0.0*	-8.3	-7.2	4.0
47. DAIRY PRODUCTS	10.0	18.6	28.0	.3*	-8.6	-18.0	9.6
48. FISH PRODUCTS	4.1	3.6	4.6	3.8	.5	-.5	.4
49. PROCESSED FOODS	8.8	9.2	19.5	9.6*	-.4	-10.7	-.8
50. FEED MEAL AND FLOUR	3.5	2.3	3.0	2.8*	1.2	.5	.7
51. WHEAT FLOUR, MALT STARCH	8.4	3.9	21.0	5.5*	4.5	-12.6	2.9
52. CEREAL PRODUCTS	9.1	3.7	21.5	7.8	5.4	-12.4	1.3
53. CONFECTIONARY PRODUCTS	12.3	7.7	27.1	9.5	4.6	-14.8	2.8
54. BEET, PULP AND SUGAR	8.6	10.1	41.9	5.4	-1.5	-33.4	3.2
55. SUGAR REFINERY PRODUCTS	14.4	12.3	39.7	5.2	2.1	-25.3	9.2
56. LIQUOR AND BEER	10.7	9.0	19.7	22.3	1.7	-9.0	-11.5
57. ALCOHOL AND WINE	14.0	15.4	29.9	26.9	-1.3	-15.9	-12.9
58. TOBACCO, PROCESSED	25.9	41.2	254.9	42.8	-15.3	-229.1	-16.9

TABLE 10 continued

CLASSIFICATION	TARIFF IN				CANADIAN TARIFF LESS TARIFF IN		
NO. VERBAL NAME	CANADA	U.S.	JAPAN	E.E.C.	U.S.	JAPAN	E.E.C.
59. RUBBER PRODUCTS	11.2	11.3	14.0	10.2	-.1	-2.8	1.0
60. LEATHER	7.7	3.9	7.8	2.7	3.8	-.1	5.0
61. RUBBER PRODUCTS	9.7	9.7	10.3	7.7	.0	-.6	2.0
62. LEATHER GOODS	15.3	13.5	13.3	9.9	1.8	2.0	5.4
63. TEXTILE PRODUCTS, COTTON	15.8	11.7	10.5	12.5	5.1	6.3	4.3
64. YARN OF WOOL HAIR	11.6	18.3	5.6	7.3	-6.8	5.9	4.3
65. TEXTILE PRODUCTS, WOOL	14.5	24.7	9.9	10.3	-10.2	4.6	4.2
66. TEXTILES SILK AND SYNT.	10.6	16.3	10.3	9.5	-5.6	.3	1.1
67. TEXTILE PRODUCTS N.E.S.,M	19.6	16.1	15.1	13.0	3.4	4.5	6.6
68. TEXTILE PRODUCTS N.E.S.,M	16.7	14.4	10.9	10.6	2.4	5.8	6.2
69. FUR	11.3	14.0	22.5	8.8	-2.8	-11.3	2.4
70. WOOD PRODUCTS,E	8.3	5.9	9.3	5.8	2.4	-1.0	2.5
71. WOOD PRODUCTS,M	5.3	3.8	4.1	4.0	1.5	1.2	1.2
72. WOOD PRODUCTS,M	13.5	10.6	11.2	8.4	2.9	2.3	5.1
73. PULP AND PAPER PRODUCTS,E	4.4	4.1	8.3	6.6	.3	-3.9	-2.2
74. PULP AND PAPER PRODUCTS,M	9.0	7.1	10.6	9.3	1.9	-1.6	-.3
75. PULP AND PAPER PRODUCTS,M	11.1	7.9	10.1	10.0	3.2	1.0	1.1
76. PRINTING	8.5	4.0	3.7	4.9	4.6	4.8	3.7

TABLE 10 continued

CLASSIFICATION		TARIFF IN			CANADIAN TARIFF LESS TARIFF IN		
NO. VERBAL NAME	CANADA	U.S.	JAPAN	E.E.C.	U.S.	JAPAN	E.E.C.
77. IRON AND STEEL INTERMED	7.3	8.4	9.2	7.2	-1.1	-1.8	.1
78. GRAPHITE AND CARBON	6.6	4.7	5.4	4.6	1.9	1.3	2.1
79. IRON AND STEEL INTERMED,M	4.8	5.8	6.7	5.2	-.9	-1.8	-.4
80. IRON AND STEEL INTERMED,E	4.8	5.5	7.8	4.8	-.7	-3.0	.1
81. NONFERROUS METAL PROD.,E	3.6	5.8	8.4	3.5	-2.2	-4.8	.1
82. NONFERROUS METAL PROD.,M	10.8	8.7	10.2	7.9	2.1	.6	2.9
83. NONFERROUS METAL PROD.,E	8.6	9.3	10.1	6.4	-.7	-1.5	2.2
84. PLUMBING MISC.EQUIP.	12.3	8.0	9.2	7.8	4.3	3.1	4.5
85. AGRICULTURAL MACHINERY	6.5	4.0	8.6	6.0	2.5	-2.1	.5
86. OTHER MACHINERY AND EQUIP.	8.3	6.9	9.2	6.6	1.3	-1.0	1.7
87. AIRCRAFT INC. PARTS	4.2	5.3	11.8	6.0	-1.1	-7.7	-1.8
88. AUTOS, TRUCKS AND PARTS	3.7	5.7	14.5	12.2	-2.0	-10.8	-8.5
89. BUSES AND LOCOMOTIVES	8.3	7.9	13.3	9.7	.4	-4.9	-1.4
90. TRANSPORTATION EQUIPMENT	2.3	3.2	4.0	1.8	-.9	-1.7	.5
91. ELECTRICAL APPLIANCES	9.4	8.7	9.5	8.0	.7	-.1	1.4
92. ELECTRICAL EQUIPMENT	9.0	8.3	13.5	10.5	.7	-4.6	-1.5
93. MINERAL PRODUCTS,E	6.9	6.6	6.5	5.2	.3	.3	1.6
94. MINERAL PRODUCTS,M	8.8	14.6	8.0	7.7	-5.8	.8	1.1
95. PETROLEUM PRODUCTS,M	3.5	6.1	9.8	4.2	-2.6	-6.3	-.7
96. PETROLEUM PRODUCTS,M	6.1	6.1	16.2	6.1	-.0	-10.1	-.0

TABLE 10 continued

CLASSIFICATION NO.	VERBAL NAME	TARIFF IN				CANADIAN TARIFF LESS TARIFF IN		
		CANADA	U.S.	JAPAN	E.E.C.	U.S.	JAPAN	E.E.C.
97.	NAPHTHA AND ASPHALT	5.6	3.8	5.0	2.6	1.8	.6	3.1
98.	COAL PRODUCTS N.E.S.	2.9	3.0	4.7	1.6	-.2	-1.8	1.3
99.	EXPLOSIVES	13.0	7.1	13.4	7.0	5.9	-.4	6.0
100.	PHARMACEUTICALS	7.5	7.5	9.4	6.5	.0	-1.9	1.0
101.	CHEMICALS	3.1	3.4	5.3	4.2	-.3	-2.3	-1.2
102.	INORGANIC CHEMICALS,M	8.9	7.7	9.6	6.9*	1.2	-.7	2.0
103.	INORGANIC CHEMICALS,E	6.3	7.9	9.9	8.2	-1.6	-3.5	-1.8
104.	INDUSTRIAL CHEMICALS	8.4	10.5	9.8	5.9	-2.1	-1.4	2.5
105.	SCIENTIFIC EQUIPMENT	7.5	11.7	9.4	9.0	-4.2	-2.0	-1.6
106.	JEWELRY	11.1	12.4	13.0	7.7	-1.3	-1.9	3.4
107.	PLASTICS PRODUCTS	11.2	10.1	10.8	8.4	1.1	.4	2.8
108.	END PRODUCTS N.E.S.,M	14.3	11.1	10.9	9.1	3.1	3.4	5.2
109.	END PRODUCTS N.E.S.,M	6.0	4.6	5.1	3.5	1.4	.9	2.5

obstructing trade. There is an extensive literature on this subject which is much too large to review here, except for a brief comment (Stegeman, 1973; Grey, 1973). In one respect, non-tariff barriers represent a spectrum. At one end are measures applying across the board to many or all commodities; at the other end are non-tariff barriers applying to specific commodities. The latter are the most relevant for this study. The specific type of non-tariff barrier protecting a particular commodity is applied with greatest frequency and force to Agricultural resources, liquor and beer, and textiles. Often the application of the tariff is so severe that discussion of the tariffs themselves is irrelevant.

In the earlier part of this study, we took note of some of the Agricultural resources Canada was able to export despite foreign trade barriers. These include Live animals (1), Wheat (3), Honey and beeswax (7) and Oil seed and oil nuts (11). Similarly, a number of Agricultural resources are primarily imported despite the Canadian tariff. This implies that Canadian production is at a higher cost than in the rest of the world. These include some items in the following classifications: Eggs (6), Nuts, fruits and berries (8), Vegetables (9), Hay, grass and nursery (10), and Hops (12). In the cases of Milk (5) and Tobacco (13), non-tariff barriers are so obstructive that nothing can be deduced from 1961 trade figures, although Canada is generally considered to have a comparative disadvantage in the production of Milk (5) and a comparative advantage in the production of Tobacco (13) (Report of the Task Force on Agriculture, 1969, chap. 9, A). Economic considerations (as opposed to non-economic arguments) would imply that, in the interest of world specialization and efficiency, foreign tariff and non-tariff barriers should be reduced on the Agricultural resources exported by Canada and that Canada should make corresponding reductions in tariff and non-tariff barriers applying to imported Agricultural resources. This would shift the Canadian productive effort out of high-cost lines of production and into lines where she has a comparative advantage, thus reducing the costs of producers of processed foods and the prices of consumers.

Of the Forestry resources, we found that Logs and bolts (16) and Pulpwood (18) accounted for a considerable proportion of the cost of Canadian commodity exports. Logs and bolts (16) were imported into Canada in 1961 over a small tariff of about 2.9 per cent. Canada's tariff in the four Forestry resource classifications are higher than in the EEC, the United States, or Japan. The Canadian tariffs on energy are higher than the United States and the EEC, but lower than Japan (see classifications 26 to 29 in Table 10). Energy is a net export from Canada, but because of transportation costs energy is both imported and exported. If foreign tariffs are lower than the Canadian tariff, this raises the cost of processing in Canada above the foreign cost. This point could be of significance to Ontario. The tariff schedule, however, makes special provision for a number of firms using coal for smelting, synthetic rubber production, evaporating to produce salt, and other productive uses.

Perhaps the group of foreign tariffs which work most against Canadian commodity exports are the Japanese tariffs, which apply to the agricultural processing classifications (49 to 58), and the EEC variable import duties. Canadian Agricultural resources are exported particularly through Feed meal and flour (50) and Wheat flour, malt and starch (51), and Japanese tariffs in these categories are higher than that applied in other regions.

GENERAL EFFECTS OF THE TARIFF

Table 11 was prepared to test the relationship between the variables in Table 9 and the tariff data of Table 10. The entries in these tables are coefficients of correlation between the variable noted in the row and the variable noted in the column. For example, the correlation between Forestry resource costs (row 2) and the US tariff (column 2) is −0.068.

In examining these tables, a question of interpretation arises which makes it necessary to specify a critical value of the sample correlation coefficient. Below the critical value the correlation is considered to be so weak as to suggest the absence of any 'true' correlation. Above the critical value of the correlation it is considered strong enough to permit us to conclude that the sample correlation arises because there is a corresponding correlation in the 'economic universe' from which the data are assumed to be 'drawn.'[1]

The choice of a value of r_o for the sample correlation coefficient as the critical value (demarcating significant values from non-significant values) is based upon a standard expression relating the square of the correlation coefficient to the student's t distribution as indicated below (Christ, 1960, 517):

$$r^2 = t^2 / (t^2 + n - 2). \tag{3}$$

---

1 Since all 80 groups are observed, it might seem at first that conventional tests of significance are not relevant. This type of situation occurs frequently in quantitative analysis of socioeconomic data (and especially in conjunction with the use of time-series.) The usual approach is to adopt a statistical model in which an underlying relationship is assumed. The underlying relationship incorporates unobservable random terms. In this context, we must acknowledge that these random terms may in part account for the observed correlations; and had these unobservable random terms assumed values different from those observed in fact, the observations on our variables would have been different from what is actually reported. In this sense, the data constitute a sample from an underlying universe.

TABLE 11

Correlation between tariffs in Canada, US, EEC and Japan with selected variables

NAME OF VARIABLE	TARIFF ON ALL ITEMS				THE CANADIAN TARIFF LESS THE TARIFF IN			TARIFF ON DUTIABLE ITEMS				WEIGHTED AVERAGE TARIFF IN CANADA LESS TARIFFS IN		
	CAN. (1)	U.S. (2)	JAPAN (3)	E.E.C. (4)	U.S. (5)	JAPAN (6)	E.E.C. (7)	CAN. (8)	U.S. (9)	JAPAN (10)	E.E.C. (11)	U.S. (12)	JAPAN (13)	E.E.C. (14)
1. AGRICULTURAL RESOURCES	.082	.278	.300	.113	-.379	-.312	-.072	.011	.350	.306	.130	-.474	-.343	-.201
2. FORESTRY RESOURCES	.045	-.068	.021	.019	.158	.028	.003	.043	-.058	-.019	.033	.141	.032	.019
3. MINERALS AND METALS	-.177	-.047	-.068	-.063	-.029	.059	-.001	-.019	-.065	-.067	-.062	.064	.071	.073
4. ENERGY RESOURCES	-.163	-.128	-.048	-.124	-.009	.020	-.015	-.086	-.082	-.045	-.118	-.003	-.029	.053
5. IMPORTED RESOURCES	.347	.210	.131	.115	.131	-.074	.265	.244	.204	.130	.114	.048	-.085	.221
6. TOTAL RESOURCES	-.072	.093	.176	-.013	-.271	-.207	-.072	-.044	.182	.186	.013	-.315	-.222	-.097
7. WAGE COSTS	.196	.053	-.146	.053	.190	.199	.168	.201	.001	-.151	.039	.274	.222	.277
8. OTHER VALUE ADDED	-.256	-.138	.085	-.099	-.273	-.164	-.303	-.303	-.081	.091	-.083	-.301	-.180	-.374
9. (8) EXCLUDING RESOURCE V.A.	-.288	-.285	-.154	-.103	-.090	.111	-.209	-.257	-.336	-.160	-.116	.118	.115	-.241
10. INTERMEDIATE GOODS PURCHASES	.617	.251	.205	.159	-.133	-.182	.028	.224	.301	.212	.174	-.114	-.182	.088
11. INTERMEDIATE GOODS SHIPMENTS	-.312	-.290	-.271	-.315	.064	.235	.096	-.196	-.237	-.271	-.320	.064	.256	.208
12. DIRECT PLUS INDIRECT PURCHASES OF INTERMEDIATE GOODS	.233	.281	.211	.245	-.164	-.185	-.087	.277	.319	.217	.257	-.067	-.175	.036

To obtain the critical value r_o, we insert the critical value of t in (3) after first deciding a level of statistical significance. Thus, if we choose a two-tailed test at the 10 per cent level of significance, the critical t-values will be ±1.66 (approximately) for a sample size of 80. We then obtain the critical value $r_o \cong 0.186$.

Thus if we obtain a sample correlation of, say, $r = -0.23$, we would conclude that since this is numerically larger than 0.186, the sample value is not simply a chance result from an underlying population or universe in which there is an actual correlation of zero, but rather that the correlation is derived from a universe in which there is a true correlation between the variables. On the other hand, a sample value such as ±0.08 would be insufficiently large numerically to permit the conclusion that it provides evidence for the existence of correlation.

In the preceding section it was determined that Canada succeeds in exporting Agricultural resources but that the value of them required to produce Canadian commodity exports is less than the amount it would cost to purchase the Agricultural resources required to produce Canadian imports. In this sense, Canada is a net importer of Agricultural resources through commodity trade. Above we established the point that this was, in part, because Canadian agriculture is more highly specialized. From Table 11 we see that it may also be due to the structure of tariffs.

Reading across row 1 of Table 11, we determine that the tariff in the United States and Japan is higher on a processed commodity the greater the percentage of the total production cost of a commodity that is used to purchase Agricultural resources. The correlations with tariffs computed from all items (columns 2 and 3) and with tariffs computed from dutiable items only (columns 9 and 10) are positive and significant in the case of the United States and Japan, but the Canadian and the EEC correlations are not significant. These latter two correlations and the correlations using the US and Japanese tariffs are consistent with the hypothesis that those tariff schedules are biased against the processing in Canada of Agricultural resources, while the EEC tariffs are neutral. Moreover, the US and Japanese tariffs rise relative to the Canadian tariff as the value of Agricultural resources in the commodity increases. Columns 5 to 7 and 12 to 14 report on the correlation between the proportion of cost spent on Agricultural resources and the difference between the foreign and Canadian tariff. The negative correlations imply that the higher the foreign tariff relative to the Canadian tariff applied in a commodity classification the greater the cost of Agricultural resources required in proportion to the total cost of producing such commodities. The correlation is more strongly established when based on the dutiable tariff items. The negative correlations for the United States and Japan, in columns 12 and 13 are numerically larger than the correlations in columns 5 and 6, and even the EEC correlation is significant when based on the dutiable tariff items (see column 14).

Reading across row 2 of Table 11 one finds no significant correlations. The tariff is not higher in commodity groups in which the proportion of Forestry resources in the total cost of commodities is high. Similarly, row 3 shows consistently small correlations between the various tariff rates and the porportion of the total cost expenditure used to purchase Metals and minerals. Interestingly, these are all negative, but none are significant. This is also true of the Energy resource costs reported in row 4, except that the negative correlations are numerically larger.

The correlations on line 5 suggest that tariffs rise the greater the proportion of the total cost of a commodity that is required to purchase imported resources, but only the Canadian and US correlations are significant. From columns 7 and 14 we see that the Canadian tariff rises significantly relative to the EEC. The correlation implies that Canada is attempting to capture processing of a category of resources which cannot be produced in Canada at all. In so far as these resources are goods required jointly in the processing of Canadian resources, the tariff must raise the cost of producing the Agricultural resources that Canada in fact produces with a comparative advantage. Thus, in attempting to capture the processing of foreign resources, Canada increases the cost of processing Canadian resources.

Line 6 reports on correlations between the cost of all resources taken together and the various tariffs in Table 10. With the tariffs based on all items there are no significant correlations between the tariff and the proportion of resource costs in the total costs of a commodity. There is a significant correlation, however, between the level of the Canadian tariff relative to the US and Japanese tariffs. The negative correlations imply that the Canadian tariff tends to rise relative to the US and Japanese tariffs as the proportion of Canadian resources in the cost of a commodity increases (see line 6, columns 5, 6, 12, and 13). Commodities with relatively high resource costs represent earlier stages of processing. To the extent that Canada protects these, she is operating contrary to her frequently avowed intention to use tariffs as a means of extending the level of processing. In connection with Table 10 we noted that Canada's tariffs on Forestry resources tended to be higher than in the rest of the world.

In terms of the three major resource groups it would appear that the Canadian tariff protects commodities where Wage cost is high relative to Other value added. From lines 7 to 9 in columns 1 and 8 of Table 11, we see that the Canadian tariff rises as the Wage cost rises and falls as Other value added rises. These are significant correlations. The negative correlation between the Canadian tariff and the resource-intensiveness of commodities (line 6, columns 1 and 8) is not significant. However, the correlations in row 6, columns 5, 6, 12, and 13, are significant. The Canadian tariff declines relative to the foreign tariff the greater the resource-intensiveness of the commodity. Considering these correlations, it would seem reasonable to characterize the effects of the Canadian tariff as providing protection to labour-intensive commodities relative to capital-intensive ones and as neutral with respect to resources.

Rows 10, 11, and 12 reconfirm a basic proposition concerning tariffs. In all nations the tariff rises with the degree of processing. Row 10 displays the correlations between various tariffs and the intermediate goods required in the production of a commodity. The greater the purchases of intermediate goods, the greater the tariff in all regions. Row 11 shows that tariffs are lower for commodities that ship most of their output to other producers. The higher the ratio of intermediate goods shipped to total supply, the lower the tariff. Row 12, the concept of backward linkage, is the same conceptually as line 10 except that in calculating the use of intermediate goods in an industry both direct and indirect purchases were included. The distinctions between these various measures of the stage of processing are irrelevant, however, because the correlations on lines 10 to 12 all lead to the same conclusion. Each region provides greater protection the closer we approach the end-product stage.

CONCLUSIONS

1 In both the United States and Japan industries receive greater tariff protection the greater the percentage of total costs used to purchase Agricultural resources. This is not true of the EEC tariff, but it was noted that the Japanese tariff was relatively high in certain classifications of particular significance to Canada.
2 There is no significant correlation between the levels of Canadian, Japanese, EEC, or US tariffs and the percentage of cost used to purchase Forestry resources, Minerals and metals, or Energy resources.
3 There is evidence that Canada attempts to capture processing of resources which are not produced in Canada. In so far as these are used jointly to produce intermediate products, it increases the cost of processing Canadian resources at later stages and increases the cost of producing end products.
4 The Canadian tariff tends to protect labour-intensive commodities. This must shift production away from Canada's comparative advantage, which is based on her ample supply of land resources.
5 The tariff increases with the degree of processing in all regions considered.

4
Ontario's stake

One occasionally hears expressed the view that the Canadian tariff has contributed more to the economic development of Ontario than it has to other provinces. The statement cannot refer to the effects of the tariff on per capita income, because, as noted in the introduction, empirical research has demonstrated that, under the tariff, income per capita is less than it would be in free trade. The statement probably refers to the growth of manufacturing in Ontario relative to agriculture or to the assumed expansion of production of end-products relative to intermediate products. It has never been confirmed by empirical evidence that the tariff has this effect. The empirical evidence of Table 11 does confirm the *intent* to favour production of end products in Canada (and in other nations), but the evidence in this study indicates that this intention has not succeeded in establishing end-product production at a level that would be achieved in free trade. The empirical evidence assembled here would favour the hypothesis that the tariff has encouraged agricultural production in Ontario relative to agricultural production in the rest of Canada and that it has expanded intermediate processing in Canada at later stages relative to production of end products. These, in combination, have the effect of reducing the level of processing and manufacturing in Ontario.

In the first chapter, Canadian commodity trade was characterized in terms of its effect on supply and demand for resources. In terms of the cost of producing commodities, Canada could be described as exporting resources in exchange for labour and other value added. But we soon determined that this proposition had to be examined at a more disaggregated level because the Canadian resource base is quite specialized.

AGRICULTURAL RESOURCES

In the nomenclature of this study, three classifications account for most of Canada's net exports of Agricultural resources: Live animals (1), Wheat (3), and Oil seeds and oil nuts (11). These tend to be produced relatively more outside Ontario. Because they are exported from Canada, the Canadian tariff and non-tariff barriers are comparatively ineffective in raising Canadian prices relative to foreign prices. This is exactly the opposite of the situation which exists with regard to imported Agricultural resources. These include items in Milk (5), Eggs (6), Nuts, fruits and berries (8), Vegetables (9) and Hay, grass and nursery (10). In these categories the Canadian tariff and non-tariff barriers can be effective in raising Canadian prices and hence can encourage production above the free trade level. With the exception of Hay, grass and nursery (10), these tend to be produced relatively more in Ontario, which therefore benefits to a greater extent from the tariff protection of Canadian agriculture.

The protection of Canadian Agricultural resources that are import-competing also explains in part why processing in Ontario would be greater in free trade. The food processing industry benefits from the efficient production of some fruits and vegetables in Ontario, but tariff and non-tariff barriers raise the cost of Agricultural resources complementary in processing. We noted in the earlier sections that Canada does not, on net, export Agricultural resources as part of the value of commodities. This must be recognized as partly the consequence of a policy intended to maintain a broadly-based Canadian production at the resource stage.

It was determined from the correlation analysis in Table 11 that Canada was notable in attempting to process Agricultural resources not produced in the country. From the earlier analysis it was determined that there were net imports of these into Canada as part of the value of processed commodities over the Canadian tariff. This implies that Canada has a comparative disadvantage in processing these imported resources. By establishing high-cost production at certain stages of processing, Canada reduces the competitiveness of processing at other stages. Such protection adds to the cost of processing the Agricultural resources produced in Canada with comparative advantage. There were seven Non-competing agricultural resources defined in this study: Rice (2), Raw cotton (120), Rubber (121), Cane sugar (122), Cocoa beans (123), Green coffee (124), and Tropical fruit (125).

The effect of protecting the processing of Non-competing agricultural resources will be illustrated with the case of Cane sugar (122). Sugar is on the import control list, and there are a number of rather complicated tariff items in the Canadian schedule which protect the Sugar refinery industry.[1] Data for the Sugar refinery industry and other industries using sugar are listed in Table 12. The list consists of all food processing industries where Ontario's share of Value added and employment are above the median for manufacturing. Each is concerned with processing Canadian agricultural resources, but the potential to compete with imports and, in the case of Distilleries, the potential to export are reduced to the extent that the tariff protecting the Sugar refinery industry increases the cost of intermediate goods produced from sugar.[2]

Table 12 is intended to illustrate a general point. In attempting to capture the processing of resources produced outside Canada the government increases the cost of processing Canadian resources. There is an inevitable tradeoff in which one producer group is sacrificed to another. The government implicitly decides to protect one stage of processing at the expense of others, having no regard for economic efficiency, the Canadian resource base, or the cost to the consumer. Economists have long advocated the strategy that Canada should import at that stage of processing where foreign production is less costly than Canadian and export at stages where Canada has a comparative advantage.

TEXTILES

A similar situation exists with regard to production of clothing. Raw cotton (120) and Rubber (121) are not produced in Canada, and Wool in the grease (15) is imported. Which stages of processing, if any, should be protected? The simulation analysis summarized in chapter 2 leads to the conclusion that in the textile sector the tariff has succeeded in extending production toward later stages of processing, but in most textile industries Value added and employment tends to be located outside Ontario. Ontario has relatively little at stake, and Canada as a whole has much to lose from further expansion of the textile industry. Low-income families spend a greater proportion of their budget on textiles than do high-income families, so that low-income families are affected more adversely by higher prices. Furthermore, wages are generally lower in the textile industry. It is important to keep in mind (recall the arguments made in the introduction) that one cannot reduce imports of textiles without adversely affecting the export sector of the economy, which is efficient by international standards.

---

1 This is explained in part by Canada's policy of protecting sugar beet production, which is another example of the general policy of maintaining a broadly-based Canadian production at the resource stage.
2 There are tariff items through which some processers are able to import at lower duty or no duty.

TABLE 12

Ontario's share of value added and employment in four food processing industries, 1965-70, and trade, 1970

1960 SIC	Ratio: Ontario/Canada Value added 1	Employment 2	Trade/ Output 3
(112) Fruit and vegetable canners	0.61	0.57	−0.12
(133) Sugar refineries	L	L	−0.01
(125) Breakfast cereal mfg	G	G	−0.01
(131) Confectionery manufacturers	0.65	0.58	−0.14
(143) Distilleries	0.63	0.54	+0.42
(147) Wineries	0.72	0.69	−0.58

NOTE: L means less than the median; G means greater than the median.

TABLE 13

Ontario's share of employment and value added, 1965-70, and trade, 1970, in industries processing forestry products

1960 SIC	Ratio: Ontario/Canada Value added 1	Employment 2	Trade/ Output 3
(251) Sawmills	0.10	0.12	0.52
(252) Veneer and plywood mills	0.15	0.19	0.13
(254) Sash and door and planing mills	0.35	0.33	0.07
(256) Wooden box factories	0.68	0.61	−0.01
(258) Coffin and casket industries	0.33	0.34	0.00
(259) Miscellaneous wood industries	L	L	−0.08
(261) Household furniture industries	0.49	0.48	−0.04
(264) Office furniture industries	0.66	0.60	0.03
(266) Other furniture industries	0.46	0.41	−0.02
(271) Pulp and paper mills	0.27	0.29	0.66
(272) Asphalt roofing manufacturing	0.41	0.39	−0.02
(273) Paper box and bag manufacturing	0.50	0.50	−0.04
(274) Other paper converters	0.67	0.67	−0.11

NOTE: L means less than the median.

FORESTRY RESOURCES

Unlike Agricultural resources, Forestry resources conform to the general Canadian pattern. Forestry resources are exported from Canada in unprocessed form and also as part of the cost of commodities. The resource stage includes Logs and bolts (16) and Pulpwood (18). As the reader may confirm from Table 13, the industrial classes principally using these tend to be located relatively more outside Ontario. The median ratio of Ontario value added to Canadian value added in a Standard Industrial Classification manufacturing category is 0.53, and the median ratio for employment is 0.50. With some exceptions, the industries listed in Table 13 report ratios lower than this. This would suggest that Ontario has less interest than other provinces in tariffs relating to Forestry resources. The reader will note also from the trade ratios in column 3 of Table 13 that import competition is present in all industries where the Ontario share (as indicated in columns 1 and 2) is greater than 0.5. On the other hand, where Ontario has a smaller share the industry is export-oriented. With general tariff reductions there should be some necessary adjustment in the Canadian import-competing industries. These are relatively more located in Ontario. There will also be some expansion of the export sector but this is located outside Ontario. Areas outside of Ontario will benefit more from lower foreign duties. This shift should be in accordance with regional and international specialization and constitutes efficient adjustment of Canadian resources and labour.

MINERALS

According to Table 6, minerals play a small role in trade. There were four classifications of substantial export of minerals: Sulphur (30), Asbestos (31), Gypsum (32), and Salt (33). Sulphur (30) is used principally by Pulp and paper mills, and its abundance in Canada helps to establish this export classification (see Table A2). Asbestos (31) and Gypsum (32) find their greatest use in the industries listed in Table 14. These are heavier products which do not enter international trade in volume, and with one exception the ratio of employment in Ontario to employment in Canada as a whole is below the median for manufacturing. The effects of tariff changes in Ontario through the mineral industries should be no greater than the effects elsewhere in Canada.

METALS

The point was made in connection with Table 7 that Metal ores (22) is the resource classification most important to Canada's commodity exports. From Table 15 we see that Ontario has much more at stake than the rest of Canada in the metals industries. In terms of Value added or employment, the Ontario share is greater than 0.5 in all the industries listed except Boiler and plate works, Smelting and refining, and Fabricated structural metals. Of the industries listed, (295), (297), and (298) are associated with Metal ores (22), while the remainder are associated with Iron ores (24). From the ratio of trade to output, we determine that

TABLE 14

Ontario's share of value added and employment, 1965-70, and trade, 1970, in industries processing asbestos and gypsum

| 1960 SIC | Ratio: Ontario / Canada | | Trade/ Output |
	Value added 1	Employment 2	3
(272) Asphalt roofing manufacturing	0.41	0.39	−0.02
(341) Cement manufactures	0.35	0.31	0.05
(343) Lime manufactures	0.54	0.53	0.06
(345) Gypsum products manufacturing	0.36	0.40	−0.01
(347) Concrete products manufacturing	0.49	0.48	0.02
(348) Ready mix concrete manufacturing	0.37	0.38	0.00

TABLE 15

Ontario's share of employment and value added, 1965-70, and trade, 1970, in industries processing metals

| 1960 SIC | Ratio: Ontario / Canada | | Trade/ Output |
	Value added 1	Employment 2	3
(291) Iron and steel mills	0.84	0.78	0.04
(292) Steel pipe and tube mills	0.64	0.66	−0.18
(294) Iron foundries	0.74	0.74	−0.17
(295) Smelting and refining	0.22	0.35	1.05
(297) Copper and alloy rolling, casting and extruding	0.61	0.62	0.21
(298) Metal rolling, casting and extruding, NES	0.75	0.76	0.18
(301) Boiler and plate works	0.50	0.49	−0.02
(302) Fabricated structural metal industry	0.49	0.45	0.01
(303) Ornamental and architectural metal industry	0.56	0.50	0.00
(304) Metal stamping, pressing and coating industry	0.62	0.59	−0.02
(306) Hardwood, tool and cutlery manufacturers	0.71	0.72	−0.22

industries based on Metal ores (22) have penetrated (successfully) the export markets of other nations while those based on Iron ores (24) meet stiff import competition or are isolated in the domestic market. Canada and Ontario have not succeeded in exporting commodities based on Iron ores (24) to the extent that one would anticipate, given her relative abundance of Iron ores (24).

It is true, of course, that the location of the processing of Iron ores (24) must depend in a complicated way on transportation costs in shipping energy and Iron ores (24) to the point of processing and on the cost of shipping the processed commodity to market. The trade data establish the point that, at the stage of smelting, Canada is competitive in world markets. Trade patterns confirm that, to the stage where Iron ores (24) are combined with energy, Canada has a comparative advantage. But what has been the effect of the tariff at later stages of processing?

The point was established in Table 11 that, regardless of how the degree of processing is defined, Canada and all other nations attempt to protect end-product industries by escalating tariffs. The simulation study referred to above would imply that in fact this has not succeeded in Canada, that under free trade the earlier stages of processing would operate at higher levels relative to the later stages. The tariff raises prices of products at the earlier stages relative to end stages and makes it more difficult for the end-stage producers to compete with imports, even with present levels of tariff protection. Also, it must be considered that at the end stage of processing, there is greater product differentiation and trade tends to flow in both directions. At high levels of Canadian and US tariffs, firms located in Canada are worse off than they would be under free trade because the firms located in the United States can achieve economies of scale on the basis of market opportunities in that country alone without the Canadian market. This is not true in the case of Canadian firms, which therefore operate at higher cost.

Let us now examine the metals industries. It was asserted above that in these the Canadian tariff has the effect of shifting the stage of processing backwards. In defining the classifications we gave consideration to the trade status and stage of processing of commodities assigned to the same classification. Consequently, in Table 16 there are three categories of Non-ferrous metal products, for example, and three categories of Iron and steel intermediate products. Column 1 is the Canadian tariff level for 1970, columns 2, 3, and 4 are the three alternate measures of 'degree of processing.' Column 2 is the amount of resources purchased directly to produce one dollar of output. Column 3 is the amount of resources purchased directly and indirectly per dollar of output. Column 4 is the ratio of intermediate shipments of goods per dollar of total supply. Column 5 is the ratio of trade to Canadian production. Column 6 is the change in the level of output predicted by the simulation to which we earlier referred, translated in terms of the nomenclature of this study. The results of the simulation indicate all but two of the end-product classes of metal processing would expand in free trade. With the exception of Graphite and carbon (78) in the intermediate processing classifications the expansion predicted increases the farther we advance toward end-stage processing as defined in columns 2 and 3. Of perhaps greatest importance from Ontario's point of view, all classifications of Non-ferrous metals would expand. The reader will verify from Table 15 that these

TABLE 16

Tariffs and resource use in the metal products classification

Classification	1970 Canadian tariff 1	Resource cost per dollar		Ratio: Intermediate to total shipments 4	Ratio: Trade to Canadian production 5	Change in the level of output 6
		Direct only 2	Direct plus indirect 3			
Intermediate iron						
(78) Graphite and carbon	6.6	0.21	0.36	1.00	−0.35	−10.0
(80) Iron and steel intermediate	4.8	0.20	0.33	1.00	+0.50	−10.0
(79) Iron and steel intermediate	4.8	0.09	0.21	1.00	−0.01	+1.75
(77) Iron and steel intermediate	7.3	0.07	0.19	1.00	−0.18	+0.56
Intermediate non-ferrous metals						
(81) Non-ferrous metal products	3.6	0.42	0.66	0.99	+0.53	+0.082
(83) Non-ferrous metal products	8.6	0.16	0.40	0.92	+0.06	+0.152
(82) Non-ferrous metal products	10.8	0.00	0.17	0.93	−0.19	+10.00
Minerals						
(93) Mineral products	6.9	0.09	0.20	1.00	+0.02	−0.31
(94) Mineral products	8.8	0.06	0.15	0.87	−0.45	−3.2
End products						
(90) Transportation equipment	2.3	0.00	0.08	0.30	−0.12	+10.0
(87) Aircraft including parts	4.2	0.00	0.07	0.99	−0.23	+10.0
(85) Agricultural machinery	6.5	0.00	0.09	0.97	−0.92	−10.0
(86) Other machinery and equipment	8.3	0.01	0.10	0.92	−0.87	−10.0
(88) Autos, trucks and parts	3.7	0.00	0.08	0.41	−0.45	+10.0
(91) Electrical appliances	9.4	0.00	0.09	0.63	−0.37	+10.0
(92) Electrical equipment	9.0	0.00	0.17	0.60	−0.04	+10.0
(89) Buses and locomotives	8.3	0.00	0.10	0.85	−0.24	+4.6
(84) Plumbing, miscellaneous equipment	12.3	0.00	0.12	0.97	−0.45	−0.50

commodities are among the most important to Ontario in terms of Value added or Employment. The results of the simulation are corroborated by the earlier analysis, in which it was established that Canada has an exportable surplus of Metal ores (22), and further that the value of the Metal ores (22) required to produce Canada's exports of processed commodities exceeds the value of Metal ores (22) required to produce her imports of processed commodities. This would support the hypothesis that Canada has a comparative advantage in producing such commodities.

A FINAL NOTE ON THE QUESTION OF PROCESSING

Since most of the classifications in Table 16 are import-competing, it may seem strange that output in so many would increase in free trade. Would they not face even more import competition after losing the protection of the Canadian tariff? The counterarguments have already been developed above: tariffs at all stages of processing add to the Canadian cost of production. This is easily seen in financial terms, but it is not generally understood that the tariff generates a load of inefficiency for the sector as a whole which manifests itself in higher costs at all stages of processing but pyramiding particularly onto the later stages. The output of each industry depends on the cost of production in every other industry, and since the later stages of processing, by definition, purchase in greatest proportion from earlier stages, they are most affected. Ultimately, the inefficiency manifests itself in reduced purchasing power and hence diminished Canadian demand for the output of Canadian industry.

Because the commodities in Table 16 are import-competing, the Canadian tariff is the cause of cost distortion, but the foreign tariff also plays a key role. The classifications in Table 16 are heterogeneous, so that trade will flow in both directions at greater than average volume. Earlier studies have indicated that Ontario is well located geographically to compete successfully in North America (see Wonnacott and Wonnacott, 1967), and under free trade one would anticipate greater intra-industry specialization with gains in efficiency from economies of scale. The Autopact with the United States has demonstrated that Ontario products can compete on the world market if producers have access to intermediate goods at world prices.

The Canadian tariff has not contributed to the economic development of Ontario even in the sense of establishing relatively more processing than in the rest of Canada. The tariff may have had the effect of protecting Ontario agriculture relative to agriculture outside Ontario, but to the extent that it has succeeded it has raised prices of agricultural resources and worked against the growth of food processing in Ontario and Canada. The food processing industry must also be adversely affected by the attempt to establish processing in Canada of agricultural resources which cannot be grown in Canada at all, such as cane sugar. The protection of textile production appears to have succeeded in its objective of extending processing, but this has a comparatively small impact in Ontario relative to the rest of Canada. Ontario producers most successful in international competition are those engaged in producing Non-ferrous metal products. Foreign tariff reductions on these products would lead to relatively greatest expansion in Ontario.

Iron and steel processing presents Ontario with its greatest policy dilemma. Measured in terms of value added or employment, one finds that this sector is located more in Ontario than elsewhere. It is largely an import-competing sector, which therefore is dependent on the Canadian tariff for protection. Since, however, the output of this sector is concentrated on intermediate products, the tariff raises the costs of other producers who could otherwise compete more successfully against imports or penetrate further into foreign markets. The tariff protection in the iron and steel sector is passed on as higher costs in the minerals and metals sector and to the end-product stages.

The data lead this author to conclude that, contrary to the currently accepted opinion, the tariff does not succeed in shifting the stage of processing toward end products in Canada, nor does it increase manufacturing in Ontario relative to the rest of Canada. If this conclusion is corroborated by other avenues of research, we must conclude that the rationale for Canada's tariff should be reconsidered. Our study indicates that Ontario can benefit from tariff negotiations which lead toward freer trade and to that extent it is in agreement with the position taken by the Economic Council of Canada.[3]

3 The Economic Council of Canada takes the position that the benefit to Canada would derive largely from increased efficiency through economies of scale — a point which economic research has consistently supported; see Economic Council of Canada (1975).

Mathematical calculations

Many of the computations in the text are summations obtained from matrices based on input-output equations. Let a_{ij} be the amount of the ith resource or commodity required to produce one dollar's worth of j. Let n be the number of such commodities. Let b_{1j} be the amount of wages paid per dollar of output of commodity j, b_{2j} be the amount of other value added paid per dollar of output, x_{oj} be the output level of resource or commodity j, u_{ok} be the amount of total wages ($k = 1$) or other value added ($k = 2$), and f_{oj} be the level of final demand for commodity j.

If there are three commodities, the following input-output relationship holds identically:

$$\left[\begin{array}{ccc|cc} 1 - a_{11} & -a_{12} & -a_{13} & 0 & 0 \\ -a_{21} & 1 - a_{22} & -a_{23} & 0 & 0 \\ -a_{31} & -a_{32} & 1 - a_{33} & 0 & 0 \\ \hline -b_{11} & -b_{12} & -b_{13} & 1 & 0 \\ -b_{21} & -b_{22} & -b_{23} & 0 & 1 \end{array}\right] \left[\begin{array}{c} x_{01} \\ x_{02} \\ x_{03} \\ u_{01} \\ u_{02} \end{array}\right] = \left[\begin{array}{c} f_{01} \\ f_{02} \\ f_{03} \\ 0 \\ 0 \end{array}\right] . \qquad (1.1)$$

This may be expressed in matrix notation for the general case of n commodities. Let R be the matrix on the left-hand side of expression (1.1) and let $v_o' = (x_{01}, \ldots, x_{on}, u_{01}, u_{02})$ and $y_o' = (f_{01}, \ldots, f_{on}, 0, 0)$; then

$$Rv_o = y_o,$$
$$v_o = R^{-1}y_o. \qquad (1.2)$$

For notational purposes, let $Q = R^{-1}$ and let q_{rs} be an element of Q. The element q_{rs} is interpreted as the amount of resource or commodity r required directly and indirectly to produce one unit of s for final demand: $\partial x_{or}/\partial f_{os} = q_{rs}$. The elements $q_{n+1,s}$ and $q_{n+2,s}$ are respectively the amounts of wages and other value added required directly and indirectly to produce one dollar's worth of commodity s: $\partial u_{o1}/\partial f_{os} = q_{n+1,s}$ and $\partial u_{o2}/\partial f_{os} = q_{n+2,s}$.

The coefficients of Table A2 are defined as the percentage of the total amount of resource r used in Canadian commodity processing, which is used specifically in the production of commodity s. Let $s \in \Psi$ be the set of s which designate commodities, then

$$q_{rs}f_{os} \Big/ \sum_{s \in \Psi} q_{rs}f_{os} \tag{1.3}$$

are the percentages shown in Table A2. In Table 1 the above percentages are obtained by summing in the numerator and demoninator of (1.3) over the relevant ranges of r to get the aggregated resource percentages. Column 8, Labour, is obtained when we set $r = n + 1$ and column 9, Other value added including resource value added, is obtained when we set $r = n + 2$.

In column 10 the amount of Other value added excluding resource value added is computed in the following manner. Commodities 1 to 39 (excluding 2) are considered Canadian resources; therefore, $q_{n+2,s}$ ($s = 1, \dots, 39$, but $s \neq 2$) are amounts of Other value added required directly and indirectly in the production of one unit of resource output. The column elements q_{rs} ($r = 1, \dots, 39$, but $r \neq 2$) for any $s \in \Psi$ are the direct plus indirect requirements of Canadian resources needed to produce one dollar of commodity s. The value added in the resource industries required to produce commodity s is therefore

$$\sum_{r \in \theta} q_{n+2,r} q_{rs} y_{os}, \tag{1.4}$$

where $r \in \theta$ is the set of index numbers $r = 1, \dots, 39$, but $r \neq 2$. This must be subtracted from $q_{n+2,s} y_{os}$ to obtain Other value added excluding resource value added for commodity s. In column 10 of Table 1 this is shown as a percentage of like magnitudes for all commodities.

If desired, we could compute the amount of Other value added in the resource industries required to produce the final demand vector y_o. This magnitude would be

$$\sum_{r \in \theta} \sum_{s \in \Psi} q_{n+2,r} q_{rs} y_{os}, \tag{1.5}$$

which must then be subtracted from

$$\sum_{s \in \Psi} q_{n + 2,s} y_{os}$$

to obtain the other Value added excluding resource value added.

To compute the direct plus indirect value of resource r required to produce commodity exports, replace the vector y_o in expression 2 with the vector y_e^* defined as follows. Let y_{es} be the amount of resource or commodity s exported; then the vector y_e^* has the component zero if y_{es} is a resource, and the component y_{es} itself if s is a commodity. Using (2) we obtain the vector v_e^*, whose sth component is v_{es}^*. If s is a resource, v_{es}^* is the amount of it required directly and indirectly to produce commodity exports. Similarly, one can compute $v_m^* = R^{-1} y_m^*$, where y_m^* is the vector of commodity imports. It then follows that v_{ms}^* (a component of v_m^*) is the amount of resource or commodity s required directly or indirectly to produce imports. The v_{es}^* and v_{ms}^* are aggregated over appropriate ranges to get the magnitudes shown on line B of Tables 2, 3, and 4. The Forestry resource costs appearing under imports on line 2B, for example, is $\sum_{s=16}^{20} v_{ms}^*$. The amount of Wages exported, shown on line 7B in these tables, is $v_{e, n+1}^*$ and the amount of Other value added imported shown on line 8B is $v_{m, n+2}^*$.

On line 9 of Table 2, Other value added excluding indirect resource value added is computed following closely the method described above. Recall that $q_{n+2, r}$ $(r = 1, \ldots, 39; r \neq 2)$ are the amounts of Other value added required directly and indirectly to produce one dollar of resource r. The amount of resource r required to produce commodity s exports in the amount y_{es} is $q_{rs} y_{es}$. The value added in the resource industries required indirectly to produce commodity exports is therefore as shown in (5) with y_{es} replacing y_{os}. This must be subtracted from $v_{e, n+2}^*$ to get Other value added excluding resource value added on line 9 of Tables 2, 3, and 4. The comparable magnitude for imports is obtained by substituting y_{ms} in expression 5.

In Tables 2, 3, and 4, there are magnitudes on line A which indicate the amount of resources shipped directly or through other resources. Direct shipment of Live animals (1), for example, are y_{e1}. By summing y_{es} for all Forestry resources we obtain direct exports, but we must add to the resources exported directly the amount shipped as part of the cost of other resources. Define the vector y_e^{**}, which will have the component zero if y_{es} is a commodity and will be y_{es} itself if it is a resource. Compute $v_e^{**} = R^{-1} y_e^{**}$. Let the sth component of v_e^{**} be v_{es}^{**}. If s is a resource, it is the amount required directly and indirectly to produce other resources. The v_{es}^{**}, which are Forestry resources, are added to the y_{es} exported directly to get the items on line 2A, column 1, of Tables 2, 3, and 4. The other lines denoted A are similarly computed.

Tables 5, 6, and 7 of the text and A3 through A7 of the appendix require very little additional explanation. The v_{es}^* and v_{ms}^* $(s \in \theta)$ are resource exports and imports through the value of commodities. The magnitudes in columns 3 and 4 are respectively

$$v_{es}^* \Big/ \sum_{s \in \theta} v_{es}^*,$$

$$v_{ms}^* \Big/ \sum_{s \in \theta} v_{ms}^*. \qquad\qquad (s \in \theta)$$

The index in column 3 of Table 5 is simply

$$\frac{v_{es}^* + v_{ms}^*}{v_{es}^* - v_{ms}^*}, \qquad\qquad (s \in \theta)$$

and the ratio in column 4 is

$$\frac{v_{es}^* - v_{ms}^*}{y_{es} - y_{ms}}. \qquad\qquad (s \in \theta)$$

Finally, the magnitudes shown in column 9 of Tables 5, 6, and 7 are

$$\frac{y_{es} + y_{ms}}{y_{es} - y_{ms}}. \qquad\qquad (s \in \theta)$$

The magnitudes in columns 1 and 2 of Table 9 are described in chapter 2. The percentage of cost spent directly on resources, which appears in column 3 of Table 9, is $\sum_{i \in \theta} a_{ij}$, and that spent on intermediate goods is $\sum_{i \in \psi} a_{ij}$ (column 4). Column 5 was also explained in chapter 2. The direct plus indirect purchases of domestic resources appearing in column 6 is computed as the sum $\sum_{r \in \theta} q_{rs}$. Non-competing resource purchases required directly and indirectly to produce commodity s are obtained by summing q_{rs} over values of r which are non-competing resources. These appear in column 7 of Table 9. Finally, to obtain the direct plus indirect purchases of other goods shown in column 8, we take the magnitude $\sum_{r \in \psi} q_{rs}$.

APPENDIX 2

Tables

TABLE A1

Definitions of 125-level commodities in terms of 644-level commodities
and the import commodity code

125-LEVEL CLASSIFICATION	644-LEVEL CLASSIFICATION	IMPORT COMMODITY CLASSIFICATION
NO. VERBAL NAME	CLASSIFICATION NUMBERS	CLASSIFICATION NUMBERS
1 LIVE ANIMALS	1-4,6	119,199,249,349,419-449,
		630-699,910-999
2 RICE	7	6144,6149
3 WHEAT	8	6199S
4 OTHER GRAIN	9	6129,6139,6199S
5 MILK	10	5119S
6 EGGS	11	5319
7 HONEY AND BEESWAX	12	5509,39405
8 NUTS,FRUITS,BERRIES	13,14	7103,7106,7111,7112,7117,7118,
		7130-7136,7142,7145,7150,7151,
		7159S,7163-7189,8110-8199
9 VEGETABLES	15	9105-9199
10 HAY,GRASS AND NURSERY	16-18	15572,21101-21199,21303-21399
11 OIL SEEDS,OIL NUTS	19	21230-21299
12 HOPS	20	14415
13 TOBACCO	21	18110-18299S
14 FUR	5,22,31	739,799,20220-20236,20239S,
		20245-20289
15 WOOL IN THE GREASE	23	24209
16 LOGS AND BOLTS	25	23129-23179,23859S
17 POLES AND PIT PROPS	26	23855,23859S
18 PULPWOOD	27	23869S
19 OTHER CRUDE WOOD	28	23899
20 CUSTOM FORESTRY	29	N/A
21 FISH LANDINGS	30	3021-4999S
22 METAL ORES	32	25210,25230,25339S,25825,
		25840,25875,25878S,25899S
23 RADIO-ACTIVE ORES	33	25899S
24 IRON ORES	34	25120
25 GOLD AND PLATINUM ORES	35,36	25899S
26 COAL	37	26105-26169
27 CRUDE MINERAL OILS	38	26410,26499S
28 NATURAL GAS	39	26431
29 OTHER BITUMINOUS	40	26499S
30 SULPHUR	41	27977S
31 ASBESTOS	42	27903
32 GYPSUM	43	27940
33 SALT	44	27968,27970
34 PEATMOSS	45	21999S

TABLE A1 continued

125-LEVEL CLASSIFICATION	644-LEVEL CLASSIFICATION	IMPORT COMMODITY CLASSIFICATION
NO. VERBAL NAME	CLASSIFICATION NUMBERS	CLASSIFICATION NUMBERS
35 CLAY AND OTHER REFRACT.	46	27210-27299
36 ABRASIVES	47	27410-27499
37 NON-METALLIC MINERALS	48	26432,27905-27930,27952,27965,
		27977S,27980,27985,279999S
38 SAND AND GRAVELS	49	27510,27549
39 STONE	50	27610-27699
40 SERVICES TO AGRICULTURE	24	N/A
41 SERVICES TO MINING	51	N/A
42 MEAT	52,54-56,59,64,66	1109-1155,1159S,1309-1399,
		1519,1595,1599S,1703,1709,
		1780,1799S,14440-14450
43 MARGARINE AND SHORTENING	57,58	12049,12099,39115-39199
44 HIDES AND SKINS	62	20110-20199
45 CRUDE ANIMAL PRODUCTS	53,60,61,63	1159S,15699S,20973,20976S,
		20999S
46 POULTRY PROCESSED	65	1165-1198
47 DAIRY PRODUCTS	67-74	5119S,5129S,5139S,5146,5159,
		5169S,5199S,10149S,20910
48 FISH PRODUCTS	76	3021-4999S,15660,15699S,20970,
		20976S,20999S,21999S,39229,
		39299,39449S
49 PROCESSED FOODS	75,77-86,93,99,	5359,5369,6215-6250,6299S,
	100,106-109,	6520,6549S,6699S,6920,
	112-115,117-119	6930-6999,7212-7659,7699,
		7806-7899,8210-8225,8230,
		8240-8299,9205-9799,9805-9899,
		9915-9970,9999S,10499S,
		11140-11199,11220-11249,
		11310-11349,11420-11499,11749,
		14159S,14299S,14320-14329,
		14399,14409,14410,14420,14431,
		14435,14476,14499,14636,14646,
		14650,14699S,15320-15399,
		15577S,15599S,15699S,17199S,
		17299,39308S,39312S,39316S,
		39320S,39324S,39336S,39340S,
		39344S,39348S,39352S,39360S,
		39385S,39399S,39559,39599S,
		41163-41181,41199S,42999S

TABLE A1 continued

125-LEVEL CLASSIFICATION		644-LEVEL CLASSIFICATION	IMPORT COMMODITY CLASSIFICATION
NO.	VERBAL NAME	CLASSIFICATION NUMBERS	CLASSIFICATION NUMBERS
50	FEED MEAL AND FLOUR	87-91	15519,15577S,15599S,15675
			15709,15769,15799S
51	WHEAT FLOUR,MALT STARCH	92,94,97,110	62998,64998,15577S
52	CEREAL PRODUCTS	95,96,98	15998,6417,6419,6430,6455,
			64998,6630,66998
53	CONFECTIONARY PRODUCTS	101,102,116	10402,10405,10416,10420,
			104998,14681
54	BEET,PULP AND SUGAR	103,111	10110,101918,155998
55	SUGAR REFINERY PRODUCTS	104,105	101498,10168,10170,101918
56	LIQUOR AND BEER	120,121,123,124	15539,17220,17310-17360,173998
57	ALCOHOL AND WINE	122,125	17230,17250,407998
58	TOBACCO,PROCESSED	126-128	18110-182998,18325,18330,
			18350,18399
59	RUBBER PRODUCTS	129,130	62105,625298,62549,79040-79049
60	LEATHER	144	291998,30110-30699
61	RUBBER PRODUCTS	131-143	29185,32104,32115,32119,32304,
			32313,32316,32509,32516,32520,
			32532,32536,32540,32546,32549,
			32599,38732,38736,38739,42260,
			42290,49210,49221,492408,
			49314,49316,49329,493398,
			494498,49485,494898,49691,
			62109,62115,62120,621298,
			621498,62525,625298,62539,
			786858,84492,904998,915648,
			949998,96118,96125,96129
62	LEATHER GOODS	145,147-149	30820,30899,49220,492408,
			49247,49272,78952,78959,
			79012-79039,79099,86404,86499,
			866408,867168,96104,96109
63	TEXTILE PRODUCTS,COTTON	150-155,167,169,	24440,24499,29119,36021,36049,
		170	36402,36405,36411-36499,36719,
			367898,37302-37398,38109,
			38149,38156,38159,389998,
			846338,846398,84645,84805,
			84807,848108,848398,849998,
			96151,961598
64	YARN OF WOOL HAIR	156	36320-36390

TABLE A1 continued

125-LEVEL CLASSIFICATION	644-LEVEL CLASSIFICATION	IMPORT COMMODITY CLASSIFICATION
NO. VERBAL NAME	CLASSIFICATION NUMBERS	CLASSIFICATION NUMBERS
65 TEXTILE PRODUCTS,WOOL	157-159,168,178, 179	24219-24299,36089S, 37203-37249,37703-37749,38176, 84633S,84639S,96154
66 TEXTILES,SILK AND SYNT.	160-166,171	24340,24617-24699,36259, 36609S,36619,36639,36699S, 36789S,36795,37107,37149, 37509-37599,37759-37789,37799, 38189,38191,42349S
67 TEXTILE PRODUCTS N.E.S.	174-176,180,182, 183,185-187,189, 190,195-197,199, 200-204	36914-36999,37415,37440,37449, 38119,38161,38169,38199, 38319-38399,38511,38539,38549, 38559,38599,38609,38619,38639, 38702-38729,38760-38795,38902, 38911,38919,38979,38999S, 49447,49449S,49487,49489S, 49601,49604,49699S,78119, 78149S,78199S,78304-78314, 78319,78323-78337,78341-78399, 78618-78649,78664,78665, 78685S,78689,78876,78877, 78899,78921,78999S,84412-84485 84499S,95075,95072,96157S, 96159S
68 TEXTILE PRODUCTS N.E.S.	146,172,173,177, 184,188,191-194, 198,205,206,208,	24510-24599,31039-31089,31099, 36505-36549,36903,36905,49620, 49640,60599S,72039S,74074S, 74099S,78465-78499, 78522-78549,78651,78680,78902, 78904,78999S,84501,84503, 84505,84510,84601,84650, 84699,84711S,84715,84728, 84739,84839S,84999S,86739S, 88010,88012,88019S,88027S, 88054,96159S
69 FUR	207	78809
70 WOOD PRODUCTS	209-212,215	23869S,33104-33195,33409, 33439,33499S,33513-33599, 33999

TABLE A1 continued

125-LEVEL CLASSIFICATION	644-LEVEL CLASSIFICATION	IMPORT COMMODITY CLASSIFICATION
NO. VERBAL NAME	CLASSIFICATION NUMBERS	CLASSIFICATION NUMBERS
71 WOOD PRODUCTS	214,217,219,221	33499S,33595,33902-33991, 339995,95066
72 WOOD PRODUCTS	213,216,218,220, 222-228	29199S,33609,33635,33699, 681435,698995,74012-74019, 74029,74032,74038,74039, 74042,74049,74069,74072, 74076,740995,763895,765995, 86216,86720,902995,949115, 94933,949395,95055,96139
73 PULP AND PAPER PRODUCTS	229-231,238,239, 242	34019-34095,35181,35184, 351995,40856,479995,49440, 49444,86632
74 PULP AND PAPER PRODUCTS	234,236,240,246, 247	29139,35440,35471,35499,55540, 55549,35591,55719,35760,35779, 35805-35849,366995,39915, 399455,46904,49409,789995, 880195
75 PULP AND PAPER PRODUCTS	232,233,235,237, 241,243-245, 248-250	35233-35299,35325-35399,555915 35610-35699,35749,35911-35999, 84720,848105,84924,85066, 867165,90119,90124,90128,90149 90423,90424,915645,915695, 95040,95044,95047,950495, 950795,950895,95096,950995, 96149
76 PRINTING	251-255,258	52646,52650,52651,52653,52655, 52659,83701,89104,89108,89129, 89304-89349,89403-89490, 89520-895995
77 IRON AND STEEL INTERMED	259,264,266,268, 269,273,274,276, 278,298,300,302, 303-307	44109-44199,44502-44516,44518, 44519,445205,44522,44529, 44532-44538,44542,44555, 44559-44599,44605-44630,44650, 44675,44680,44690,44807,44823, 44827-44829,44831,44836,44845, 44879,44887,44888,448995, 46113-46129,461995, 46851-46859,46910,46960,46963,

TABLE A1 continued

125-LEVEL CLASSIFICATION	644-LEVEL CLASSIFICATION	IMPORT COMMODITY CLASSIFICATION
NO. VERBAL NAME	CLASSIFICATION NUMBERS	CLASSIFICATION NUMBERS
		46999,50119,50149,52299S,
		65103S,65129S,94911S,94915
78 GRAPHITE AND CARBON	271,272	43941,47714-47732
79 IRON AND STEEL INTERMED	262,263,265,267,	44302-44350,44355,44359,
	270,275,277,299,	44505-44599,44739,44769,44799,
	301,339,340	44839,46972,55399,59299S
80 IRON AND STEEL INTERMED	260,261	44219-44255,44260,44290
81 NON-FERROUS METAL PROD	279-283,288,289,	25199,25249,25339S,25878S,
	291,293-295,308,	25899S,29199S,40205,
	311	40209-40231,40261-40299,44811,
		45109S,45204,45208-45218,
		45275S,45299S,45309,45349S,
		45415S,45469,45499,45649,
		45704,45710S,69899S,74099S,
		76389S
82 NON-FERROUS METAL PROD	290,296,297,309,	**44911-44969,45105,45109S,**
	310,312-314,	**45119-45140,45149,45710S,**
	316-330,333	**45730-45749,46135-46150,**
		46173,46199S,46502-46549,
		46553-46569,46582,46599S,
		46620-46699,46710-46739,46759,
		46908,46912,46952,46959,46967,
		52377-52396,52425S,61199S,
		65371S,65389S,69875,69899S,
		75204-75299,75408-75449,
		75510-75595,76308,76399S,
		85007,85011,85013,85019,85024,
		85039S,86716S,86732,86739S,
		86792,86799,90499S,94929S,
		94958,95005,95019,95024,95029,
		95089S
83 FERROUS METAL PROD	284-287,292,315,	40499S,45275S,45278,45285,
	331,332	45288,45299S,45512-45599,
		45608,45940-45999,46315-46399,
		75817S,75820,75822,75823,
		75865,75866,75899,85069,
		86219
84 PLUMBING MISC EQUIP	334-338,341-349	46809-46848,46879,46899,49340,

TABLE A1 continued

125-LEVEL CLASSIFICATION	644-LEVEL CLASSIFICATION	IMPORT COMMODITY CLASSIFICATION
NO. VERBAL NAME	CLASSIFICATION NUMBERS	CLASSIFICATION NUMBERS
		65103S,65129S,65149,65199,
		65212,65215,65249S,65339,
		65371S,65430-65449,661898,
		66199S,66289S,66299S,67109,
		67129,67160S,67173S,67199S,
		67219,67299S,70342,70344S,
		70395S,72044,72049,72054,
		72059S,74059,76399S,
		85044-85049,86724,93001-93016,
		93099S,95015
85 AGRICULTURAL MACHINERY	350,351	54109-54699,55103-55199
86 OTHER MACHINERY AND EQUIP	352-366,383-385,	46605,46609,50209S,50218-50229
	387	50239S,50299S,50401-50499,
		50509-50595,50733-50799,
		50804-50895,50904-50940,50969,
		50979-50999,51019-51039,
		51042-51099,52101-52199,
		52204-52252,52299S,52301-52369
		52414,52415,52425S,52448-52499
		52515-52590,52604-52645,52648,
		52657,52669,52706-52999,57119,
		57129,57157,57158,57509,
		57519-57559,57628,57699,
		59227-59255,59299S,59309,59339
		65249S,65506-65528,65554-65590
		65599S,69215S,69229S,69232,
		69762,69769,70982,70989,709935
		70996S,70998S,70999S,72069,
		73019,73029,73040-73049,73059S
		73063-73099S,75102-75198,
		77104-77199,96168,96169
87 AIRCRAFT INC. PARTS	368-371	60151-60159,60329-60349,60599S
88 AUTOS,TRUCKS AND PARTS	372,373,375-377,	58104-58149,58304-58338,58447,
	379-381	58448,58454,58499,58739,587998
		58804-58849,58919-58990,58999S
		68908-68995
89 BUSES AND LOCOMOTIVES	374,378,382	46575,58729,58909
90 TRANSPORTATION EQUIPMENT	386,388-390	58799S,59158,59169,59199S,
		61187,61199S,86790

TABLE A1 continued

125-LEVEL CLASSIFICATION	644-LEVEL CLASSIFICATION	IMPORT COMMODITY CLASSIFICATION
NO. VERBAL NAME	CLASSIFICATION NUMBERS	CLASSIFICATION NUMBERS
91 ELECTRICAL APPLIANCES	391-395,397-399,	49516,49542-49599,50209S,
	401-409,412-414	50299S,50309-50379,52345,
		52349,63519-63549,63603-63625,
		63688,63689,63699S,63919,63929
		63972-63999,65324,65329,65331,
		65353,65369,65371S,65389S,
		65392-65599,65541-65546,65599S
		66115,66159,66189S,66195,66199S
		66211,66219,66289S,66299S,
		68119,68143S,68165-68199,
		68202-68290,68326,68379,68395,
		68423,68429S,68449S,68481,
		68499S,68859,68869,68879,69209
		69215S,69219,69229S,69329-69395
		69704,69719,69754,69756,69771,
		69772,69799,69805-69829,69835,
		69856,69899S,70927S,70928S,
		72059S,73059,76303,76306,86209
		86212,91908,91910
92 ELECTRICAL EQUIPMENT	396,400,410,411	45147,46975,63699S,63936,
		63937,63949
93 MINERAL PRODUCTS	415,416,418-421,	47202-47249,47503-47512,
	434	47599S,47609-47699,47976,47999S
94 MINERAL PRODUCTS	417,422-433,435	47104-47149,47251-47299,
		47303-47335,47353-47391,47399S
		47420-47440,47454,47456,47469S
		47499S,47907,47922,47933,47936
		47939,47945,47966,47969,47999S
		49505,49509,67160S,67168,
		67173S,67199S,67299S,85015,
		85034,85061,85062,85063,85064,
		86728,86730,95032,95036,96174,
		96179,96189
95 PETROLEUM PRODUCTS	439,441	43329,43349,43965,43999S
96 PETROLEUM PRODUCTS	436-438,440,444	40621-40623,43109,43149,
		43209-43259,43945-43959,43999S
97 COAL PRODUCTS	442,443	43909S,43920
98 COAL PRODUCTS	445,601	26189,43530,43549,43909S,
		43929,43999S

TABLE A1 continued

125-LEVEL CLASSIFICATION	644-LEVEL CLASSIFICATION	IMPORT COMMODITY CLASSIFICATION
NO. VERBAL NAME	CLASSIFICATION NUMBERS	CLASSIFICATION NUMBERS
99 EXPLOSIVES	446-449	41509,41530,41569,93019,
		93099S,94956
100 PHARMACEUTICALS	455,460-462	80061-80068,80073,80089S,
		87120-87999
101 CHEMICALS	450,453,465,466,	40099S,40115,40131,40199S,
	468-470,473,475,	40206,40373,40399S,40441,
	476,477,480,491,	40499S,40653,40942,41134,
	509,516,523	41199S,41623,41626,41631,
		41633,41639,41648,41652-41689,
		41699S
102 INORGANIC CHEMICALS	451,452,454,	39308S,39312S,39316S,39324S,
	456-459,463,464,	39336S,39340S,39344S,39348S,
	471,472,474,478,	39352S,39360S,39385S,39399S,
	479,482,494,497,	39610-39699,40003,40025,40162,
	499-502,506,508,	40199S,40202,40240,40248,40257
	510-513,517-522,	40322,40328-40371,40379-40388,
	540,541,548	40395,40399S,40401,40406,40416
		40417-40427,40445,40456-40466,
		40499S,40613,40631-40642,
		40664-40691,40699S,40721,
		40761,40763,40765,40778,40780,
		40799S,40802,40803,40804,40811
		40815,40818,40819,40839,40845S
		40859,40889S,40902,40932,
		40950-40965,40975,40979,
		40982-40994,40999S,41204-41299
		41312-41399,42302-42340,42349S
		42352-42399,42453,42454,42472,
		42479,42605-42699,42709-42762,
		42775-42799 ,42816-42899,
		42947S,42949,42966,42968,80019
		80049S
103 INORGANIC CHEMICALS	467,481,483-490,	40008,40051,40081,40099S,
	492,493,495,496,	40450,40508,40532S,40545,
	498,503-505,507,	40599,40607,40609,40659,40699S
	514,515,525,552	40705,40799S,40845S,40875,
		40889S,40999S,41129 ,41145,
		42911S,86604,86608
104 INDUSTRIAL CHEMICALS	524,526-539,	21703-21799,21945-21975,21999S

TABLE A1 continued

125-LEVEL CLASSIFICATION	644-LEVEL CLASSIFICATION	IMPORT COMMODITY CLASSIFICATION
NO. VERBAL NAME	CLASSIFICATION NUMBERS	CLASSIFICATION NUMBERS
	542-547,549-551	39415,39449S,39599S, 39716-39749,39905-39910,39920, 39935,39945S,39999,40972, 41830-41879,41882-41889,41899, 42119-42199,42210,42250,42907, 42908,42911S,42915,42917, 42922,42932-42946,42947S, 42948,42952-42972,42979,42982, 42995,42999S,80077,80079, 80089S,91979,94939S
105 SCIENTIFIC EQUIPMENT	553-557	40521,40532S,70325,70328, 70344S,70348,70362,70390, 70395S,70613-70729,70909 70919,70927S,70928S,70949, 40950,70952,70954S,70958, 70993S,70996S,70998S,70999S, 72039S,79099S,88024,88027S, 88034-88049,88052,88059,90273
106 JEWELRY	558-561	47804,47825,81017-81033,81049, 82007-82089,85052,85059S, 88027S,91111-91149,91204-91219 91513-91539,91569S,91813, 91839,91939-91949,91999
107 PLASTICS PRODUCTS	564-567	42416-42429,42477,42499, 42512-42599,49339S,67164, 76389S,84711S,85059S,85068, 86532,86549,86712,86716S, 94911S,95078,95079S,95088, 95099S,96199
108 END PRODUCTS N.E.S.	562,568-570,572, 576-580	46920,46928S,46999S,49615, 49632,49660,49699S,61108, 61116,61120,63680,76113,76124, 76149,76389S,78975,78999S, 83215-83299,83709-83789,83792, 83799,86504,86520,86536,86626, 86627,86640S,90136,90204-90280 90299S,90404,90432,90489, 90499S,90504-90549,92124-92199 94418-94499,94929S,94928

TABLE A1 continued

125-LEVEL CLASSIFICATION		644-LEVEL CLASSIFICATION	IMPORT COMMODITY CLASSIFICATION
NO.	VERBAL NAME	CLASSIFICATION NUMBERS	CLASSIFICATION NUMBERS
109	END PRODUCTS N.E.S.	563,573,574,575, 581	20529,20549,24310,24320,24330, 279998,740748,94604-94640, 94952,94954,94966-94995,949998
110	DRESSING AND DYEING	181,571	N/A
111	CONSTRUCTION	582	N/A
112	TRANSPORTATION-TRADE	583-595,600, 603-607	N/A
113	ELECTRIC POWER	599	49697
114	WATER SERVICES	602	N/A
115	COMMUNICATIONS	596-598	N/A
116	BUSINESS SERVICE	367,608-611,617, 618,620-622,628, 630	N/A
117	PERSONAL SERVICE	612-616,619, 623-627,629	N/A
118	ADVERTISING,TRAVEL	256,257,636,637	N/A
119	REPAIR,SUPPLIES,SERVICE	631-635,638	N/A
120	RAW COTTON	639	24410,24430
121	RUBBER	640	21610,21620,21649
122	CANE SUGAR	641	10115,10119
123	COCOA BEANS	642	11110
124	GREEN COFFEE	643	11210
125	TROPICAL FRUIT	644	7109,7115,7124,7139,7148,71598

TABLE A2

Percentage of the total value of production of thirty-nine resources which is used in the production of eighty commodities, 1961

COMMODITY NUMBER AND NAME	PERCENT TRADED	LIVE ANIMALS (1)	RICE (2)	WHEAT (3)	OTHER GRAIN (4)	MILK (5)	EGGS (6)	HONEY AND BEESWAX (7)	NUTS FRUITS BERRIES (8)	VEGETABLES (9)
40. SERVICES TO AGRICULTURE	.00	.09	.00	.20	.31	.01	.00	.00	.00	.00
41. SERVICES TO MINING	.00	.00	.00	.00	.00	.00	.00	.00	.00	.00
42. MEAT	-.00	57.56	.26	.27	.72	.08	.06	.08	1.00	1.73
43. MARGARINE AND SHORTENING	.01	4.14	5.36	.01	1.68	.00	.51	.30	.18	.46
44. HIDES AND SKINS	.14	1.16	.00	.01	.01	.00	.00	.00	.00	.02
45. CRUDE ANIMAL PRODUCTS	.06	.89	.00	.06	.19	.00	.00	.01	.00	.01
46. POULTRY PROCESSED	-.02	8.75	.00	.02	.04	.00	.00	.00	.25	.22
47. DAIRY PRODUCTS	.01	.15	.71	.02	.25	97.07	.80	.41	1.65	.06
48. FISH PRODUCTS	.58	.01	.00	.00	.00	.00	.00	.00	1.08	.17
49. PROCESSED FOODS	-.24	.29	50.75	5.91	15.83	.35	5.50	2.95	47.85	45.54
50. FEED MEAL AND FLOUR	.01	.21	.68	16.14	43.95	.00	.03	.03	.01	.05
51. WHEAT FLOUR, MALT STARCH	.15	.01	7.67	65.98	5.90	.00	4.28	11.39	.76	.59
52. CEREAL PRODUCTS	-.07	.00	23.91	.78	1.29	.00	1.95	8.96	.70	.14
53. CONFECTIONARY PRODUCTS	-.05	.00	5.09	.30	1.62	.01	.51	.56	2.18	.38
54. BEET, PULP AND SUGAR	.25	.01	1.95	.53	.65	.00	.18	.10	.06	.39
55. SUGAR REFINERY PRODUCTS	-.04	.00	.30	.00	.09	.00	.03	.02	.07	16.02
56. LIQUOR AND BEER	.09	.00	.07	.01	9.92	.00	.01	.00	.04	.00
57. ALCOHOL AND WINE	-.43	.00	.00	.00	.15	.00	.00	.12	6.70	.00
58. TOBACCO, PROCESSED	.06	.00	.00	.00	.00	.00	.00	13.59	.00	.00
59. RUBBER PRODUCTS	-.08	.01	.00	.00	.00	.00	.00	.00	.00	.00
60. LEATHER	.04	.00	.00	.00	.00	.00	.00	.00	.00	.00
61. RUBBER PRODUCTS	-.23	.00	.00	.00	.00	.00	.00	.06	.00	.00
62. LEATHER GOODS	-.12	.00	.00	.00	.00	.00	.00	.01	.00	.00
63. TEXTILE PRODUCTS, COTTON	-.56	.00	.00	.00	.00	.00	.00	.00	.00	.00
64. YARN OF WOOL HAIR	-.22	.00	.00	.00	.00	.00	.00	.00	.00	.00
65. TEXTILE PRODUCTS, WOOL	-.63	.00	.00	.00	.00	.00	.00	.00	.00	.00
66. TEXTILES SILK AND SYNT.	-.17	.00	.00	.00	.00	.00	.00	.00	.00	.00

TABLE A2 continued

COMMODITY NUMBER AND NAME	PERCENT TRADED	LIVE ANIMALS (1)	RICE (2)	WHEAT (3)	OTHER GRAIN (4)	MILK (5)	EGGS (6)	HONEY AND BEESWAX (7)	NUTS FRUITS BERRIES (8)	VEGETABLES (9)
67. TEXTILE PRODUCTS N.E.S.,M	-.15	.03	.00	.00	.00	.00	.00	.04	.00	.00
68. TEXTILE PRODUCTS N.E.S.,M	-.21	.11	.00	.00	.00	.00	.00	.02	.00	.00
69. FUR	-.00	.00	.00	.00	.00	.00	.00	.00	.00	.00
70. WOOD PRODUCTS,E	.41	.02	.00	.00	.00	.00	.00	.17	.00	.00
71. WOOD PRODUCTS,M	-.02	.00	.00	.00	.00	.00	.00	1.52	.00	.00
72. WOOD PRODUCTS,M	-.03	.01	.00	.00	.00	.00	.00	.57	.00	.00
73. PULP AND PAPER PRODUCTS,E	.84	.00	.00	.00	.00	.00	.00	.00	.00	.00
74. PULP AND PAPER PRODUCTS,M	-.11	.00	.06	.00	.03	.00	.01	.01	.00	.00
75. PULP AND PAPER PRODUCTS,M	-.06	.01	.00	.00	.00	.00	.00	.24	.00	.00
76. PRINTING	-.21	.00	.00	.00	.00	.00	.00	.03	.00	.00
77. IRON AND STEEL INTERMED	-.18	.01	.00	.00	.00	.00	.00	.02	.00	.00
78. GRAPHITE AND CARBON	-.35	.00	.00	.00	.00	.00	.00	.09	.00	.00
79. IRON AND STEEL INTERMED,M	-.01	.00	.00	.00	.00	.00	.00	.00	.00	.00
80. IRON AND STEEL INTERMED,E	.50	.00	.00	.00	.00	.00	.00	.00	.00	.00
81. NONFERROUS METAL PROD.,E	.53	.00	.00	.00	.00	.00	.00	.00	.00	.00
82. NONFERROUS METAL PROD.,M	-.19	.01	.00	.02	.08	.00	.00	.16	.00	.00
83. NONFERROUS METAL PROD.,E	.06	.00	.00	.00	.00	.00	.00	.01	.00	.00
84. PLUMBING MISC.EQUIP.	-.45	.00	.00	.00	.00	.00	.00	.03	.00	.00
85. AGRICULTURAL MACHINERY	-.92	.00	.00	.00	.00	.00	.00	.01	.00	.00
86. OTHER MACHINERY AND EQUIP.	-.87	.02	.18	.04	.07	.06	.02	.34	.02	.03
87. AIRCRAFT INC. PARTS	-.23	.00	.00	.00	.00	.00	.00	.00	.00	.00
88. AUTOS, TRUCKS AND PARTS	-.45	.00	.00	.00	.00	.00	.00	.01	.00	.00
89. BUSES AND LOCOMOTIVES	-.24	.00	.00	.00	.00	.00	.00	.00	.00	.00
90. TRANSPORTATION EQUIPMENT	-.12	.00	.00	.00	.00	.00	.00	.00	.00	.00
91. ELECTRICAL APPLIANCES	-.37	.01	.00	.00	.00	.00	.00	.09	.00	.00
92. ELECTRICAL EQUIPMENT	-.04	.00	.00	.00	.00	.00	.00	.00	.00	.00
93. MINERAL PRODUCTS,E	.02	.01	.00	.00	.00	.00	.00	.01	.00	.00

TABLE A2 continued

COMMODITY NUMBER AND NAME	PERCENT TRADED	LIVE ANIMALS (1)	RICE (2)	WHEAT (3)	OTHER GRAIN (4)	MILK (5)	EGGS (6)	HONEY AND BEESWAX (7)	NUTS FRUITS BERRIES (8)	VEGETABLES (9)
94. MINERAL PRODUCTS,M	-.45	.00	.00	.00	.00	.00	.00	.01	.00	.00
95. PETROLEUM PRODUCTS,M	-.23	.00	.00	.00	.00	.00	.00	.07	.00	.00
96. PETROLEUM PRODUCTS,M	-.09	.00	.00	.00	.00	.00	.00	.15	.00	.00
97. NAPHTHA AND ASPHALT	-.09	.00	.00	.00	.00	.00	.00	.01	.00	.00
98. COAL PRODUCTS N.E.S.	-.40	.00	.00	.00	.00	.00	.00	.11	.00	.00
99. EXPLOSIVES	-.02	.00	.00	.00	.00	.00	.02	.00	.02	.03
100. PHARMACEUTICALS	-.17	.10	.34	.05	.25	.00	.03	2.11	.00	.00
101. CHEMICALS	.19	.02	.00	.00	.03	.00	.00	.02	.01	.01
102. INORGANIC CHEMICALS,M	-.26	.43	.07	.00	.02	.00	.01	5.15	.00	.00
103. INORGANIC CHEMICALS,F	.03	.00	.00	.00	.02	.00	.00	.24	.02	.03
104. INDUSTRIAL CHEMICALS	-.15	.01	.43	.00	.13	.00	.04	3.16	.00	.00
105. SCIENTIFIC EQUIPMENT	-.85	.00	.00	.00	.00	.00	.00	.00	.00	.00
106. JEWELRY	-1.00	.00	.00	.00	.00	.00	.00	.05	.00	.00
107. PLASTICS PRODUCTS	-.38	.15	.00	.00	.00	.00	.00	.12	.00	.00
108. END PRODUCTS N.E.S.,M	-.35	.01	.00	.00	.00	.00	.00	5.55	.00	.00
109. END PRODUCTS N.E.S.,M	-.21	.04	.00	.00	.01	.00	.00	1.43	.00	.00
110. DRESSING AND DYEING	.00	.00	.00	.00	.00	.00	.00	.00	.00	.00
111. CONSTRUCTION	.00	.00	.00	.00	.00	.00	.00	.00	.00	.00
112. TRANSPORTATION-SPACE	.03	21.12	1.76	1.40	2.47	1.81	1.38	1.95	1.97	1.34
113. ELECTRIC POWER	.01	.00	.00	.00	.00	.00	.00	.00	.00	.00
114. WATER SERVICES	-.00	.00	.00	.00	.00	.00	.00	.00	.00	.00
115. COMMUNICATIONS	.01	.01	.00	.00	.00	.00	.00	.00	.00	.00
116. BUSINESS SERVICE	-.01	.57	.14	.18	.22	.23	72.13	33.24	29.30	28.39
117. PERSONAL SERVICE	-.06	.00	.00	.00	.00	.00	.00	.00	.00	.00
118. ADVERTISING,TRAVEL	-.00	.00	.00	.00	.00	.00	.00	.00	.00	.00
119. REPAIR, SUPPLIES, SERVICE	.09	.00	.00	.00	.00	.00	12.50	4.67	6.09	4.35
RESOURCE INDUSTRIES		7.97	.27	8.87	14.10	.38	.02	.03	.01	.02

TABLE A2 continued

COMMODITY NUMBER AND NAME	HAY AND GRASS (10)	OIL SEEDS AND NUTS (11)	HOPS (12)	TOBACCO (13)	FUR (14)	WOOL IN THE GREASE (15)	LOGS AND BOLTS (16)	POLES AND PIT PROPS (17)	PULPWOOD (18)	OTHER CRUDE WOOD (19)
40. SERVICES TO AGRICULTURE	.84	.00	.00	.00	.00	.00	.00	.00	.00	1.06
41. SERVICES TO MINING	.00	.00	.00	.00	.00	.00	.00	.00	.00	.00
42. MEAT	1.20	.36	.00	1.30	.07	.00	.03	.00	.00	1.06
43. MARGARINE AND SHORTENING	.06	.40	.05	.00	.01	.00	.00	.00	.00	.01
44. HIDES AND SKINS	.04	.00	.00	.00	.00	.00	.00	.00	.00	.05
45. CRUDE ANIMAL PRODUCTS	.03	.00	.00	.00	.00	.00	.00	.00	.00	.00
46. POULTRY PROCESSED	.11	.00	.00	.00	.00	.00	.00	.00	.00	.00
47. DAIRY PRODUCTS	.08	.24	.01	.00	.00	.00	.01	.00	.00	.25
48. FISH PRODUCTS	.00	.00	.00	.00	.00	.00	.00	.00	.00	1.12
49. PROCESSED FOODS	.03	.00	.00	.00	.00	.00	.00	.00	.00	.40
50. FEED MEAL AND FLOUR	4.03	79.93	.78	.00	.00	.00	.00	.00	.00	.01
51. WHEAT FLOUR, MALT STARCH	.02	.66	.07	.00	.00	.00	.00	.00	.00	.03
52. CEREAL PRODUCTS	.00	.37	.01	.00	.00	.00	.00	.00	.00	.07
53. CONFECTIONARY PRODUCTS	.00	5.35	.05	.00	.00	.00	.00	.00	.00	.04
54. BEET, PULP AND SUGAR	.14	.15	.02	.00	.00	.00	.00	.00	.00	.00
55. SUGAR REFINERY PRODUCTS	.00	.02	.00	.00	.00	.00	.00	.00	.00	.32
56. LIQUOR AND BEER	.00	.01	97.66	.00	.00	.00	.00	.00	.00	.00
57. ALCOHOL AND WINE	.00	.00	.30	.00	.00	.00	.00	.00	.00	.00
58. TOBACCO, PROCESSED	.00	.00	.00	98.43	.00	.00	.00	.00	.00	.00
59. RUBBER PRODUCTS	.00	.00	.00	.00	.00	.00	.00	.00	.00	.00
60. LEATHER	.00	.00	.00	.00	.00	.00	.00	.00	.00	.00
61. RUBBER PRODUCTS	.00	.00	.00	.00	.02	.00	.00	.00	.00	.02
62. LEATHER GOODS	.00	.00	.00	.00	.02	.00	.00	.00	.00	.02
63. TEXTILE PRODUCTS, COTTON	.00	.00	.00	.00	.03	.00	.00	.00	.00	.00
64. YARN OF WOOL HAIR	.00	.00	.00	.00	.13	.32	.00	.00	.00	.00
65. TEXTILE PRODUCTS, WOOL	.00	.00	.00	.00	.00	8.89	.00	.00	.00	.00
66. TEXTILES SILK AND SYNT.	.00	.00	.00	.00	.00	84.56	.00	.00	.00	.00
	.00	.00	.00	.00	.00	1.22	.00	.00	.00	.00

TABLE A2 continued

COMMODITY NUMBER AND NAME	HAY AND GRASS (10)	OIL SEEDS AND NUTS (11)	HOPS (12)	TOBACCO (13)	FUR (14)	WOOL IN THE GREASE (15)	LOGS AND BOLTS (16)	POLES AND PIT PROPS (17)	PULPWOOD (18)	OTHER CRUDE WOOD (19)
67. TEXTILE PRODUCTS N.E.S.,M	.00	.00	.00	.00	85.06	.20	.00	.00	.00	.26
68. TEXTILE PRODUCTS N.E.S.,M	.01	.00	.00	.00	6.98	4.31	.00	.00	.00	.02
69. FUR	.00	.00	.00	.00	6.26	.00	.00	.00	.00	.00
70. WOOD PRODUCTS,E	.00	.06	.00	.00	.00	.00	87.22	3.39	.02	.80
71. WOOD PRODUCTS,M	.00	.00	.00	.00	.00	.00	4.69	13.81	.13	.26
72. WOOD PRODUCTS,M	.00	.00	.00	.00	.01	.00	4.78	4.63	.00	1.02
73. PULP AND PAPER PRODUCTS,E	.44	.00	.00	.00	.00	.00	.01	.00	75.95	.42
74. PULP AND PAPER PRODUCTS,M	.06	.01	.46	.00	.00	.00	.34	.00	6.72	.05
75. PULP AND PAPER PRODUCTS,M	.19	.00	.00	.00	.01	.00	.08	.02	16.28	.21
76. PRINTING	.01	.00	.00	.00	.00	.00	.00	.00	.00	.01
77. IRON AND STEEL INTERMED	.00	.00	.00	.00	.00	.00	.00	.04	.00	.91
78. GRAPHITE AND CARBON	.00	.00	.00	.00	.00	.00	.00	.01	.00	.05
79. IRON AND STEEL INTERMED,M	.00	.00	.00	.00	.00	.00	.00	.00	.00	1.10
80. IRON AND STEEL INTERMED,E	.00	.00	.00	.00	.00	.00	.00	.00	.00	.43
81. NONFERROUS METAL PROD.,E	.00	.00	.00	.00	.00	.00	.02	.28	.00	.14
82. NONFERROUS METAL PROD.,M	.01	.00	.00	.00	.00	.00	.00	.07	.00	.02
83. NONFERROUS METAL PROD.,E	.00	.00	.00	.00	.00	.00	.00	.13	.00	.01
84. PLUMBING MISC.EQUIP.	.00	.00	.00	.00	.00	.00	.00	.09	.00	.01
85. AGRICULTURAL MACHINERY	.00	.00	.00	.00	.00	.00	.00	.32	.39	.07
86. OTHER MACHINERY AND EQUIP.	.00	.02	.02	.02	.03	.01	.17	.00	.00	.00
87. AIRCRAFT INC. PARTS	.00	.00	.00	.00	.00	.00	.00	.00	.00	.00
88. AUTOS, TRUCKS AND PARTS	.00	.00	.00	.00	.00	.00	.00	.00	.00	.01
89. BUSES AND LOCOMOTIVES	.00	.00	.00	.00	.00	.00	.00	.00	.00	.00
90. TRANSPORTATION EQUIPMENT	.00	.00	.00	.00	.00	.00	.00	.00	.00	.10
91. ELECTRICAL APPLIANCES	.00	.00	.00	.00	.00	.00	.00	.00	.00	.00
92. ELECTRICAL EQUIPMENT	.00	.00	.00	.00	.00	.00	.00	.00	.00	.00
93. MINERAL PRODUCTS,E	.00	.00	.00	.00	.00	.00	.00	.00	.00	.86

TABLE A2 continued

COMMODITY NUMBER AND NAME	HAY AND GRASS (10)	OIL SEEDS AND (11)	HOPS (12)	TOBACCO (13)	FUR (14)	WOOL IN THE GREASE (15)	LOGS AND BOLTS (16)	POLES AND PIT PROPS (17)	PULPWOOD (18)	OTHER CRUDE WOOD (19)
94. MINERAL PRODUCTS,M	.00	.00	.00	.00	.00	.00	.00	.00	.01	.82
95. PETROLEUM PRODUCTS,M	.00	.00	.00	.00	.00	.00	.00	.00	.00	.00
96. PETROLEUM PRODUCTS,M	.00	.00	.00	.00	.03	.00	.00	.00	.00	.01
97. NAPHTHA AND ASPHALT	.00	.00	.00	.00	.00	.00	.00	.00	.00	.00
98. COAL PRODUCTS N.E.S.	.00	.00	.00	.00	.00	.00	.00	.06	.00	.02
99. EXPLOSIVES	.00	.00	.00	.00	.00	.00	.00	.00	.00	.00
100. PHARMACEUTICALS	.01	.07	.16	.00	.40	.00	.00	.00	.00	.00
101. CHEMICALS	.00	.00	.00	.00	.00	.00	.00	.00	.03	.00
102. INORGANIC CHEMICALS,M	.01	10.99	.00	.00	.04	.00	.01	.00	.04	.01
103. INORGANIC CHEMICALS,E	.00	.00	.00	.00	.00	.00	.00	.00	.00	.00
104. INDUSTRIAL CHEMICALS	.00	.12	.00	.00	.00	.00	.04	.46	.00	.01
105. SCIENTIFIC EQUIPMENT	.00	.00	.00	.00	.01	.00	.00	.00	.00	.00
106. JEWELRY	.00	.00	.00	.00	.03	.00	.00	.07	.00	.00
107. PLASTICS PRODUCTS	.00	.00	.30	.00	.00	.00	.01	.43	.00	.05
108. END PRODUCTS N.E.S.,M	.00	.00	.00	.00	.07	.00	.03	.42	.00	.02
109. END PRODUCTS N.E.S.,M	.02	.00	.00	.00	.03	.00	.01	.06	.00	.05
110. DRESSING AND DYEING	.00	.00	.00	.00	.00	.00	.00	.00	.00	.00
111. CONSTRUCTION	32.83	.00	.00	.00	.00	.00	.14	74.55	.00	.00
112. TRANSPORTATION-CRUDE	3.32	.50	.37	.22	.65	.25	1.70	.21	.02	.15
113. ELECTRIC POWER	.00	.00	.00	.00	.00	.00	.01	.00	.17	.00
114. WATER SERVICES	.00	.00	.00	.00	.00	.00	.00	.00	.08	.00
115. COMMUNICATIONS	.00	.00	.00	.00	.00	.00	.00	.00	.00	.00
116. BUSINESS SERVICE	2.63	.04	.33	.04	.16	.24	.21	.69	.17	.10
117. PERSONAL SERVICE	4.10	.00	.00	.00	.00	.00	.00	.00	.00	.00
118. ADVERTISING,TRAVEL	.00	.00	.00	.00	.00	.00	.00	.00	.00	.01
119. REPAIR, SUPPLIES, SERVICE	7.24	.00	.30	.00	.00	.00	.00	.00	.00	.00
RESOURCE INDUSTRIES	42.55	.02	.00	.00	.00	.90	.45	.24	.00	86.44

TABLE A2 continued

COMMODITY NUMBER AND NAME	CUSTOM FORESTRY (20)	FISH LANDINGS (21)	METAL ORES (22)	RADIO-ACTIVE ORES (23)	IRON ORES (24)	GOLD AND PLATINUM ORES (25)	COAL (26)	CRUDE MINERAL ORES (27)	NATURAL GAS (28)	OTHER BITUMINOUS (29)
40. SERVICES TO AGRICULTURE	.12	.00	.00	.00	.00	.00	.04	.00	.04	.00
41. SERVICES TO MINING	.00	.00	.00	.00	.00	.00	.01	.00	.00	.00
42. MEAT	.00	.94	.00	.00	.01	.00	.56	.00	1.65	.00
43. MARGARINE AND SHORTENING	.00	.00	.00	.00	.00	.00	.10	.00	.19	.00
44. HIDES AND SKINS	.00	.00	.00	.00	.00	.00	.01	.00	.03	.00
45. CRUDE ANIMAL PRODUCTS	.00	.00	.00	.00	.00	.00	.01	.00	.02	.00
46. POULTRY PROCESSED	.00	.00	.00	.00	.01	.00	.04	.00	.24	.00
47. DAIRY PRODUCTS	.00	.00	.00	.00	.03	.00	.90	.00	1.10	.00
48. FISH PRODUCTS	.00	92.07	.00	.00	.00	.00	.09	.00	.05	.00
49. PROCESSED FOODS	.00	.01	.00	.00	.00	.00	1.29	.01	1.37	.00
50. FEED MEAL AND FLOUR	.00	.53	.00	.00	.00	.00	.07	.00	.30	.00
51. WHEAT FLOUR,MALT STARCH	.00	.00	.00	.00	.00	.00	.14	.00	1.21	.00
52. CEREAL PRODUCTS	.00	.00	.00	.00	.00	.00	.15	.00	1.12	.00
53. CONFECTIONARY PRODUCTS	.00	.00	.00	.00	.00	.00	.16	.00	.17	.00
54. BEEF, PULP AND SUGAR	.00	.00	.00	.00	.00	.00	.02	.00	.05	.00
55. SUGAR REFINERY PRODUCTS	.00	.00	.00	.00	.00	.00	.33	.00	.90	.00
56. LIQUOR AND BEER	.00	.00	.00	.00	.00	.00	.68	.00	.49	.00
57. ALCOHOL AND WINE	.00	.00	.00	.00	.00	.00	.03	.00	.03	.00
58. TOBACCO, PROCESSED	.00	.00	.00	.00	.00	.00	.06	.00	.03	.00
59. RUBBER PRODUCTS	.00	.00	.00	.00	.00	.00	.41	.00	.05	.00
60. LEATHER	.00	.00	.00	.00	.00	.00	.30	.00	.03	.00
61. RUBBER PRODUCTS	.00	.00	.00	.00	.00	.00	.48	.00	.10	.07
62. LEATHER GOODS	.00	.00	.00	.00	.00	.00	.11	.00	.07	.07
63. TEXTILE PRODUCTS, COTTON	.00	.00	.00	.00	.00	.00	.78	.00	.01	.00
64. YARN OF WOOL HAIR	.00	.00	.00	.00	.00	.00	.08	.00	.00	.00
65. TEXTILE PRODUCTS,WOOL	.00	.00	.00	.00	.00	.00	.27	.00	.04	.00
66. TEXTILES SILK AND SYNT.	.00	.00	.00	.00	.00	.00	.25	.00	.33	.00

TABLE A2 continued

COMMODITY NUMBER AND NAME	CUSTOM FORESTRY (20)	FISH LANDINGS (21)	METAL ORES (22)	RADIO-ACTIVE ORES (23)	IRON (24)	GOLD PLATINUM ORES (25)	COAL (26)	CRUDE MINERAL ORES (27)	NATURAL (28)	OTHER BITUMINOUS (29)
67. TEXTILE PRODUCTS N.E.S.,M	.00	.00	.00	.00	.00	.00	.46	.00	.22	.00
68. TEXTILE PRODUCTS N.E.S.,M	.00	.00	.00	.00	.00	.01	.28	.00	.22	.00
69. FUR	.00	.00	.00	.00	.00	.00	.01	.00	.01	.00
70. WOOD PRODUCTS,E	.00	.00	.00	.00	.00	.00	.06	.00	.21	.00
71. WOOD PRODUCTS,M	.00	.00	.00	.00	.00	.00	.11	.00	.12	.00
72. WOOD PRODUCTS,M	.00	.00	.00	.00	.00	.01	.38	.00	.40	.00
73. PULP AND PAPER PRODUCTS,E	.00	.00	.03	.00	.00	.00	11.66	.00	8.66	.00
74. PULP AND PAPER PRODUCTS,M	.00	.00	.00	.00	.00	.00	1.02	.00	.79	.00
75. PULP AND PAPER PRODUCTS,M	.00	.00	.00	.00	.00	.12	2.69	.00	2.21	.00
76. PRINTING	.00	.00	.00	.00	.00	.00	.12	.00	.35	.00
77. IRON AND STEEL INTERMED	.00	.00	.25	.00	38.01	.00	14.04	.00	2.23	.00
78. GRAPHITE AND CARBON	.00	.00	.40	.40	1.96	.01	.76	.00	.09	.00
79. IRON AND STEEL INTERMED,M	.00	.00	.28	.00	45.13	.33	16.73	.00	2.46	.00
80. IRON AND STEEL INTERMED,E	.00	.00	.45	.79	11.61	.01	4.24	.00	.42	.00
81. NONFERROUS METAL PROD.,E	.00	.00	83.79	85.38	.29	1.93	7.09	.00	3.70	.00
82. NONFERROUS METAL PROD.,M	.00	.00	.04	.03	.07	.01	.38	.00	2.11	.00
83. NONFERROUS METAL PROD.,E	.00	.00	3.01	3.06	.02	7.37	.30	.00	.42	.00
84. PLUMBING MISC.EQUIP.	.00	.00	.00	.00	.02	.02	.17	.00	.58	.00
85. AGRICULTURAL MACHINERY	.00	.00	.00	.00	.00	.00	.27	.00	.30	.00
86. OTHER MACHINERY AND EQUIP.	.00	.08	.35	.35	.66	.05	.88	.03	1.04	.25
87. AIRCRAFT INC. PARTS	.00	.00	.00	.00	.00	.22	.14	.00	.21	.00
88. AUTOS, TRUCKS AND PARTS	.00	.00	.00	.00	.00	.00	1.82	.00	1.10	.00
89. BUSES AND LOCOMOTIVES	.00	.00	.00	.00	.00	.00	.04	.00	.09	.00
90. TRANSPORTATION EQUIPMENT	.00	.00	.00	.00	.03	.00	.10	.00	.07	.00
91. ELECTRICAL APPLIANCES	.00	.00	.02	.01	.00	4.02	.58	.00	.89	.00
92. ELECTRICAL EQUIPMENT	.00	.00	.10	.00	.00	.24	.12	.00	.26	.18
93. MINERAL PRODUCTS,E	.00	.00	.77	.00	.00	.00	4.60	.00	6.84	28.89

TABLE A2 continued

COMMODITY NUMBER AND NAME	CUSTOM FORESTRY (20)	FISH LANDINGS (21)	METAL ORES (22)	RADIO-ACTIVE ORES (23)	IRON ORES (24)	GOLD AND PLATINUM ORES (25)	COAL (26)	CRUDE MINERAL ORES (27)	NATURAL GAS (28)	OTHER BITUMINOUS (29)
94. MINERAL PRODUCTS,M	.00	.00	.23	.00	.13	.00	1.22	.00	2.47	7.42
95. PETROLEUM PRODUCTS,M	.00	.00	.00	.00	.12	.00	.06	5.24	.18	.00
96. PETROLEUM PRODUCTS,M	.00	.00	.00	.30	.47	.00	.20	89.93	2.72	.00
97. NAPHTHA AND ASPHALT	.00	.00	.00	.00	.00	.00	.00	2.82	.09	.00
98. COAL PRODUCTS N.E.S.	.00	.00	.10	.08	.60	.00	.91	.16	.10	.00
99. EXPLOSIVES	.00	.00	.00	.00	.00	.00	.15	.00	.11	55.93
100. PHARMACEUTICALS	.00	.00	.00	.30	.00	.00	.38	.00	.26	.00
101. CHEMICALS	.00	.00	.26	.24	.10	.00	2.00	.00	2.86	1.90
102. INORGANIC CHEMICALS,M	.00	.00	.40	.79	.02	.01	1.91	.06	2.97	1.37
103. INORGANIC CHEMICALS,E	.00	.00	.14	.13	.00	1.74	.97	.00	1.36	.00
104. INDUSTRIAL CHEMICALS	.00	.00	.04	.00	.01	.00	1.58	.01	2.07	.03
105. SCIENTIFIC EQUIPMENT	.00	.00	.00	.00	.00	1.48	.06	.00	.04	.00
106. JEWELRY	.00	.00	.00	.00	.00	59.04	.05	.00	.04	.00
107. PLASTICS PRODUCTS	.00	.00	.30	.00	.03	.36	.15	.00	.18	.05
108. END PRODUCTS N.E.S.,M	.00	.00	.00	.00	.00	.58	.17	.00	.20	.00
109. END PRODUCTS N.E.S.,M	.00	.01	.00	.00	.00	7.55	.04	.03	.06	.19
110. DRESSING AND DYEING	.00	.00	.00	.00	.00	.00	.10	.00	.09	.00
111. CONSTRUCTION	.00	.00	.00	.00	.00	.00	.00	.00	.00	.00
112. TRANSPORTATION-SPACE	2.09	2.04	.03	.00	.59	4.73	3.50	.02	20.75	2.20
113. ELECTRIC POWER	.03	.00	.49	.50	.00	.01	4.18	.00	2.15	.01
114. WATER SERVICES	.00	.00	.00	.00	.00	.00	.01	.00	.01	.00
115. COMMUNICATIONS	.00	.00	.00	.00	.00	.00	.00	.00	.10	.00
116. BUSINESS SERVICE	3.17	1.82	.27	.26	.09	.60	.37	1.68	9.89	.98
117. PERSONAL SERVICE	.00	.00	.00	.00	.00	4.27	.19	.00	.77	.00
118. ADVERTISING,TRAVEL	.00	.00	.00	.00	.00	.00	.05	.00	.15	.00
119. REPAIR, SUPPLIES, SERVICE	.00	.40	.00	.30	.00	.00	.00	.00	.00	.00
RESOURCE INDUSTRIES	94.58	2.09	8.63	8.79	.00	5.26	5.36	.03	4.74	.53

TABLE A2 continued

COMMODITY NUMBER AND NAME	SULPHUR (30)	ASBESTOS (31)	GYPSUM (32)	SALT (33)	PEATMOSS (34)	CLAY AND OTHER MATERIALS (35)	ABRASIVES (36)	NON-METALLIC MINERALS (37)	SAND AND GRAVELS (38)	STONE (39)
40. SERVICES TO AGRICULTURE	.00	.00	.00	.02	1.36	.00	.00	.00	.00	.00
41. SERVICES TO MINING	.00	.00	.00	.00	.00	4.58	7.91	.40	.01	.01
42. MEAT	.00	.00	.03	9.62	.68	.00	.01	.00	.01	.01
43. MARGARINE AND SHORTENING	.02	.00	.04	.96	.00	.09	.02	.02	.02	.00
44. HIDES AND SKINS	.00	.00	.00	.19	.03	.00	.00	.01	.00	.00
45. CRUDE ANIMAL PRODUCTS	.00	.00	.00	.17	.06	.00	.00	.01	.00	.00
46. POULTRY PROCESSED	.00	.00	.00	.26	.14	.00	.00	.00	.00	.00
47. DAIRY PRODUCTS	.00	.00	.01	2.09	.12	.00	.00	.00	.00	.00
48. FISH PRODUCTS	.00	.00	.00	3.82	.00	.01	.00	.00	.00	.00
49. PROCESSED FOODS	.08	.00	.41	5.74	.00	.07	.62	.06	.00	.01
50. FEED MEAL AND FLOUR	.00	.00	.00	6.29	.00	.28	.00	.20	.00	.73
51. WHEAT FLOUR, MALT STARCH	.01	.00	.06	3.13	.00	.01	.01	.01	.06	.02
52. CEREAL PRODUCTS	.00	.00	.01	1.99	.00	.00	.00	.00	.00	.00
53. CONFECTIONARY PRODUCTS	.01	.00	.34	.31	.00	.00	.01	.01	.00	.00
54. BEET, PULP AND SUGAR	.00	.00	.02	.08	.23	.00	.04	.00	.00	.01
55. SUGAR REFINERY PRODUCTS	.04	.00	.00	.02	.00	.00	2.73	.00	.00	.33
56. LIQUOR AND BEER	.00	.00	.60	.24	.00	.00	.00	.00	.00	.00
57. ALCOHOL AND WINE	.00	.00	.00	.00	.00	.00	.00	.00	.00	.00
58. TOBACCO, PROCESSED	.00	.00	.00	.00	.00	.00	.00	.00	.00	.00
59. RUBBER PRODUCTS	.00	.00	.00	.00	.00	.44	.05	.13	.00	.00
60. LEATHER	.00	.00	.00	1.37	.00	.00	.00	.00	.00	.00
61. RUBBER PRODUCTS	1.32	2.00	.00	.00	.00	2.30	1.47	.30	.00	.03
62. LEATHER GOODS	.01	.00	.00	.01	.00	.04	.02	.00	.00	.00
63. TEXTILE PRODUCTS, COTTON	.00	.00	.00	.00	.00	.01	.00	.01	.00	.00
64. YARN OF WOOL HAIR	.00	.00	.00	.00	.00	.00	.00	.00	.00	.00
65. TEXTILE PRODUCTS, WOOL	.00	.00	.00	.01	.00	.00	.00	.00	.00	.00
66. TEXTILES SILK AND SYNT.	.33	.00	.00	.74	.00	.01	.12	.49	.00	.03

TABLE A2 continued

COMMODITY NUMBER AND NAME	SULPHUR (30)	ASBESTOS (31)	GYPSUM (32)	SALT (33)	PEATMOSS (34)	CLAY AND OTHER MATE (35)	ABRASIVES (36)	NON-METALLIC MINE (37)	SAND AND GRAVELS (38)	STONE (39)
67. TEXTILE PRODUCTS N.E.S.,M	.05	.75	.00	.00	.00	.61	.13	.09	.00	.11
68. TEXTILE PRODUCTS N.E.S.,M	.02	.10	.00	.02	.00	.22	.02	.16	.00	.01
69. FUR	.00	.00	.00	.00	.00	.00	.00	.00	.00	.00
70. WOOD PRODUCTS,E	.00	.00	.00	.00	.00	.00	.00	.00	.00	.00
71. WOOD PRODUCTS,M	.07	.01	.00	.01	.00	.08	.01	.02	.00	.00
72. WOOD PRODUCTS,M	.00	.01	.00	.00	.00	.08	.02	.01	.05	.02
73. PULP AND PAPER PRODUCTS,E	40.30	2.09	.00	3.85	.00	18.12	1.03	8.77	.10	3.12
74. PULP AND PAPER PRODUCTS,M	7.56	.20	.00	.74	.00	2.15	.09	.77	.01	.25
75. PULP AND PAPER PRODUCTS,M	9.65	7.02	.00	.83	.00	6.69	.24	2.24	.05	1.31
76. PRINTING	.01	.05	.00	.00	.00	.25	.04	.00	.00	.00
77. IRON AND STEEL INTERMED	.13	.00	.00	.00	.00	6.69	.63	1.55	.85	1.27
78. GRAPHITE AND CARBON	.04	.08	.00	.03	.00	.33	.01	.13	.02	.08
79. IRON AND STEEL INTERMED,M	.17	.00	.00	.02	.00	8.16	1.68	1.93	1.06	1.49
80. IRON AND STEEL INTERMED,E	.06	.00	.00	.03	.00	1.81	.00	.47	.10	.38
81. NONFERROUS METAL PROD.,E	4.14	.06	.30	6.04	.00	.19	.33	7.25	.05	.40
82. NONFERROUS METAL PROD.,M	.00	.08	.00	.01	.00	.19	.53	.04	.08	.01
83. NONFERROUS METAL PROD.,E	.15	.00	.00	.22	.00	.03	.05	.27	.02	.02
84. PLUMBING MISC.EQUIP.	.00	.00	.00	.00	.00	1.08	.72	.17	.36	.02
85. AGRICULTURAL MACHINERY	.00	.00	.00	.30	.00	.09	.09	.02	.08	.00
86. OTHER MACHINERY AND EQUIP.	.31	.02	.15	.18	.00	.95	29.82	.40	.63	.13
87. AIRCRAFT INC. PARTS	.01	.00	.00	.00	.00	.03	.28	.00	.01	.00
88. AUTOS, TRUCKS AND PARTS	.00	.37	.00	.00	.00	.50	.06	.11	.38	.00
89. BUSES AND LOCOMOTIVES	.00	.00	.00	.00	.00	.02	.01	.02	.01	.00
90. TRANSPORTATION EQUIPMENT	.00	.00	.00	.00	.00	.02	.02	.00	.00	.00
91. ELECTRICAL APPLIANCES	.00	.13	.00	.00	.00	.45	.37	1.18	.09	.03
92. ELECTRICAL EQUIPMENT	.01	.00	.00	.00	.00	.39	.00	.03	.00	.00
93. MINERAL PRODUCTS,E	.02	.06	50.73	.01	.00	17.92	2.94	1.89	25.82	15.23

TABLE A2 continued

COMMODITY NUMBER AND NAME	SULPHUR (30)	ASBESTOS (31)	GYPSUM (32)	SALT (33)	PEATMOSS (34)	CLAY AND OTHER MATERIALS (35)	ABRASIVES (36)	NON-METALLIC MINERALS (37)	SAND AND GRAVELS (38)	STONE (39)
94. MINERAL PRODUCTS, M	.58	75.94	41.10	.03	.00	12.96	1.34	8.92	3.51	4.83
95. PETROLEUM PRODUCTS, M	.02	.02	.00	.05	.00	.10	.01	.02	.00	.01
96. PETROLEUM PRODUCTS, M	.16	.00	.00	.63	.00	1.06	.04	.26	.01	.02
97. NAPHTHA AND ASPHALT	.02	.11	.00	.03	.00	.03	.01	.04	.00	.02
98. COAL PRODUCTS N.E.S.	.02	1.63	.00	.01	.00	.12	.02	.20	.26	.52
99. EXPLOSIVES	3.03	.00	.00	.01	.00	.00	.00	.02	.00	.00
100. PHARMACEUTICALS	.34	.00	.00	.61	.00	.69	.19	.63	.19	.03
101. CHEMICALS	8.58	.03	.00	8.73	.00	.20	3.07	23.60	.22	.83
102. INORGANIC CHEMICALS, M	5.61	.50	1.12	6.76	.00	3.23	4.37	12.47	.31	.66
103. INORGANIC CHEMICALS, E	4.22	1.06	.00	4.72	.00	.14	1.56	6.25	.04	.37
104. INDUSTRIAL CHEMICALS	6.47	.10	.35	6.33	.00	1.00	2.52	9.18	.10	.54
105. SCIENTIFIC EQUIPMENT	.00	.00	.00	.00	.00	.01	.11	.01	.02	.00
106. JEWELRY	.00	.00	.00	.00	.00	.00	.00	.00	.00	.00
107. PLASTICS PRODUCTS	.29	.54	.00	.29	.00	.20	.14	.43	.01	.05
108. END PRODUCTS N.E.S., M	.92	.28	.30	.02	.00	.39	.04	.01	.03	.20
109. END PRODUCTS N.E.S., M	.02	.70	.02	.01	.02	.18	.02	.08	.10	.13
110. DRESSING AND DYEING	.00	.00	.00	.19	.00	.00	.00	.13	.00	.00
111. CONSTRUCTION	.00	.00	.00	.00	35.25	2.57	11.94	.32	60.23	63.04
112. TRANSPORTATION-CRUDE	.94	5.96	.72	8.90	.00	1.09	2.28	1.81	1.30	1.18
113. ELECTRIC POWER	.11	.00	.01	.06	.00	.04	.01	.06	.00	.01
114. WATER SERVICES	.05	.00	.00	.01	.00	.02	.00	.02	.00	.00
115. COMMUNICATIONS	.00	.00	.00	.00	.00	.00	.00	.00	.00	.00
116. BUSINESS SERVICE	.28	.04	.65	7.62	.26	.34	1.17	.35	.87	.67
117. PERSONAL SERVICE	.00	.00	.00	.00	.00	.06	.34	.02	.06	.00
118. ADVERTISING, TRAVEL	.00	.00	.00	.00	.00	.00	.00	.00	.00	.00
119. REPAIR, SUPPLIES, SERVICE	.00	.00	.00	.90	.00	.00	.00	.00	.00	.00
RESOURCE INDUSTRIES	7.83	.17	3.94	6.73	61.90	.67	18.71	5.98	2.91	1.83

TABLE A3

Direct and indirect trade with US in thirty-nine resources — average, 1967, 1968 and 1969

NO.	NAME OF CLASSIFICATION	PERCENTAGE OF TOTAL INDIRECT RESOURCE EXPORTS (1)	RESOURCE IMPORTS (2)	INDEX OF TRADE THROUGH COMMODITIES (3)	RATIO: INDIRECT SHIPMENTS TO DIRECT SHIPMENTS (4)	INDEX OF RESOURCE TRADE (5)
1.	LIVE ANIMALS	.047	-.090	-.074	1.730	.370
3.	WHEAT	.008	-.011	.069	10.903	1.000
4.	OTHER GRAIN	.010	-.014	.052	1.519	-.627
5.	MILK	.006	-.014	-.157	R	I
6.	EGGS	.001	-.002	-.152	2.343	-.826
7.	HONEY AND BEESWAX	.000	-.000	-.337	1.526	-.462
8.	NUTS, FRUITS, BERRIES	.002	-.008	-.376	.279	-.701
9.	VEGETABLES	.004	-.015	-.424	.653	-.847
10.	HAY, GRASS AND NURSERY	.002	-.002	-.128	.266	-.282
11.	OIL SEED OIL NUTS	.004	-.022	-.503	1.558	-.850
12.	HOPS	.001	-.000	.835	1.098	-.348
13.	TOBACCO	.000	-.064	-.727	R	I
14.	FUR	.001	-.005	-.352	.125	.287
15.	WOOL IN THE GREASE	.001	-.002	-.167	3.221	.452
16.	LOGS AND BOLTS	.145	-.052	.641	61.451	-.749
17.	POLES AND PIT PROPS	.001	-.002	-.030	.331	.762
18.	PULPWOOD	.189	-.060	.674	18.872	.671
19.	OTHER CRUDE WOOD	.001	-.001	-.013	.189	.958
20.	CUSTOM FORESTRY	.040	-.014	.645	R	I
21.	FISH LANDINGS	.042	-.007	.814	1.937	.426
22.	METAL ORES	.278	-.254	.284	5.149	.180

TABLE A3 continued

NO.	NAME OF CLASSIFICATION	PERCENTAGE OF TOTAL INDIRECT RESOURCE EXPORTS (1)	RESOURCE IMPORTS (2)	INDEX OF TRADE THROUGH COMMODITIES (3)	RATIO: INDIRECT SHIPMENTS TO DIRECT SHIPMENTS (4)	INDEX OF RESOURCE TRADE (5)
23.	RADIO-ACTIVE ORES	.031	-.028	.293	98.290	1.000
24.	IRON ORES	.032	-.087	-.250	.228	.758
25.	GOLD AND PLATINUM ORES	.002	-.012	-.658	9.610	1.000
26.	COAL	.046	-.087	-.070	44.690	-.986
27.	CRUDE MINERAL OILS	.069	-.138	-.104	.238	.982
28.	NATURAL GAS	.003	-.006	-.041	.033	.592
29.	OTHER BITUMINOUS	.000	-.000	.467	.024	.500
30.	SULPHUR	.006	-.005	.312	.383	.715
31.	ASBESTOS	.002	-.006	-.373	.039	.994
32.	GYPSUM	.000	-.000	-.305	.023	.988
33.	SALT	.002	-.003	.026	.626	.117
34.	PEATMOSS	.000	-.000	-.076	.001	1.000
35.	CLAY AND OTHER	.003	-.005	-.065	2.309	-.772
36.	ABRASIVES	.001	-.005	-.417	R	-1.000
37.	NON-METALLIC MINERALS	.011	-.018	-.012	1.402	-.445
38.	SAND AND GRAVELS	.004	-.008	-.155	8.671	-.907
39.	STONE	.005	-.010	-.067	2.283	-.420

I RESOURCE EXPORTS AND IMPORTS EQUAL ZERO.

R RESOURCE EXPORTS EQUAL ZERO.

TABLE A4

Direct and indirect trade with EEC in thirty-nine resources – average, 1967, 1968 and 1969

NO. NAME OF CLASSIFICATION	PERCENTAGE OF TOTAL INDIRECT RESOURCE EXPORTS (1)	RESOURCE IMPORTS (2)	INDEX OF TRADE THROUGH COMMODITIES (3)	RATIO; INDIRECT SHIPMENTS TO DIRECT SHIPMENTS (4)	INDEX OF RESOURCE TRADE (5)
1. LIVE ANIMALS	.051	-.080	-.034	5.343	.315
3. WHEAT	.005	-.016	-.419	.007	1.000
4. OTHER GRAIN	.006	-.025	-.498	.083	.999
5. MILK	.016	-.060	-.423	R	I
6. EGGS	.001	-.002	-.414	.426	.864
7. HONEY AND BEESWAX	.000	-.000	-.579	.076	.530
8. NUTS, FRUITS, BERRIES	.002	-.032	-.829	1.133	-.369
9. VEGETABLES	.003	-.019	-.603	1.518	-.122
10. HAY, GRASS AND NURSERY	.001	-.002	-.097	.261	-.683
11. OIL SEED OIL NUTS	.004	-.029	-.659	.027	.960
12. HOPS	.000	-.001	-.814	.130	-.201
13. TOBACCO	.002	-.013	-.612	R	I
14. FUR	.001	-.007	-.634	.044	.862
15. WOOL IN THE GREASE	.001	-.008	-.714	1.636	.653
16. LOGS AND BOLTS	.096	-.029	.664	30.431	.896
17. POLES AND PIT PROPS	.001	-.002	-.261	R	I
18. PULPWOOD	.151	-.050	.638	4.684	1.000
19. OTHER CRUDE WOOD	.001	-.001	-.275	12.488	1.000
20. CUSTOM FORESTRY	.030	-.010	.627	R	I
21. FISH LANDINGS	.030	-.010	.635	.527	.914
22. METAL ORES	.429	-.189	.541	.803	.997

TABLE A4 continued

NO.	NAME OF CLASSIFICATION	PERCENTAGE OF RESOURCE EXPORTS (1)	TOTAL INDIRECT RESOURCE IMPORTS (2)	INDEX OF TRADE THROUGH COMMODITIES (3)	RATIO: INDIRECT SHIPMENTS TO DIRECT SHIPMENTS (4)	INDEX OF RESOURCE TRADE (5)
23.	RADIO-ACTIVE ORES	.049	-.021	.554	3.783	1.000
24.	IRON ORES	.016	-.088	-.584	.052	1.000
25.	GOLD AND PLATINUM ORES	.002	-.025	-.812	R	I
26.	COAL	.032	-.081	-.269	4452.167	1.000
27.	CRUDE MINERAL OILS	.043	-.130	-.342	R	I
28.	NATURAL GAS	.002	-.005	-.209	R	I
29.	OTHER BITUMINOUS	.000	-.000	.146	R	-1.000
30.	SULPHUR	.005	-.005	.230	.471	.997
31.	ASBESTOS	.001	-.008	-.737	.003	1.000
32.	GYPSUM	.000	-.000	-.743	20.063	-.340
33.	SALT	.002	-.003	-.054	731.328	-.958
34.	PEATMOSS	.000	-.000	-.312	R	I
35.	CLAY AND OTHER	.002	-.065	-.354	357.990	-.498
36.	ABRASIVES	.001	-.065	-.414	R	-1.000
37.	NON-METALLIC MINERALS	.010	-.019	-.107	.106	.983
38.	SAND AND GRAVELS	.002	-.008	-.494	47.817	-.754
39.	STONE	.004	-.010	-.325	33.175	-.968

[I] RESOURCE EXPORTS AND IMPORTS EQUAL ZERO.

[R] RESOURCE EXPORTS EQUAL ZERO.

TABLE A5

Direct and indirect trade with EFTA in thirty-nine resources – average 1967, 1968 and 1969

NO.	NAME OF CLASSIFICATION	PERCENTAGE OF TOTAL RESOURCE EXPORTS (1)	INDIRECT RESOURCE IMPORTS (2)	INDEX OF TRADE THROUGH COMMODITIES (3)	RATIO: INDIRECT SHIPMENTS TO DIRECT SHIPMENTS (4)	INDEX OF RESOURCE TRADE (5)
1.	LIVE ANIMALS	.040	-.085	-.285	14.074	.786
3.	WHEAT	.003	-.011	-.482	.020	1.000
4.	OTHER GRAIN	.004	-.015	-.565	.111	1.000
5.	MILK	.006	-.086	-.840	R	I
6.	EGGS	.000	-.002	-.495	4.096	.312
7.	HONEY AND BEESWAX	.000	-.000	-.549	.937	.473
8.	NUTS, FRUITS, BERRIES	.001	-.012	-.780	.107	.995
9.	VEGETABLES	.002	-.013	-.659	4.279	.658
10.	HAY, GRASS AND NURSERY	.001	-.002	-.423	.100	.212
11.	OIL SEED OIL NUTS	.003	-.018	-.699	.125	1.000
12.	HOPS	.000	-.000	-.562	R	I
13.	TOBACCO	.007	-.001	.750	R	I
14.	FUR	.003	-.004	-.032	.060	-.366
15.	WOOL IN THE GREASE	.003	-.002	-.105	R	I
16.	LOGS AND BOLTS	.022	-.029	-.050	119.730	.581
17.	POLES AND PIT PROPS	.000	-.002	-.598	R	I
18.	PULPWOOD	.013	-.032	-.372	R	I
19.	OTHER CRUDE WOOD	.000	-.001	-.442	R	I
20.	CUSTOM FORESTRY	.004	-.008	-.215	R	I
21.	FISH LANDINGS	.035	-.031	.142	1.051	.261
22.	METAL ORES	.691	-.368	.376	1.383	.999

TABLE A5 continued

NO.	NAME OF CLASSIFICATION	PERCENTAGE OF TOTAL INDIRECT RESOURCE EXPORTS (1)	PERCENTAGE OF TOTAL INDIRECT RESOURCE IMPORTS (2)	INDEX OF TRADE THROUGH COMMODITIES (3)	RATIO: INDIRECT SHIPMENTS TO DIRECT SHIPMENTS (4)	INDEX OF RESOURCE TRADE (5)
23.	RADIO-ACTIVE ORES	.079	-.042	.381	R	I
24.	IRON ORES	.011	-.054	-.610	3.358	1.000
25.	GOLD AND PLATINUM ORES	.001	-.019	-.837	.086	1.000
26.	COAL	.024	-.054	-.313	R	I
27.	CRUDE MINERAL OILS	.028	-.068	-.350	R	I
28.	NATURAL GAS	.001	-.003	-.329	R	I
29.	OTHER BITUMINOUS	.000	-.000	-.044	R	I
30.	SULPHUR	.002	-.003	-.191	R	I
31.	ASBESTOS	.001	-.002	.530	.006	1.000
32.	GYPSUM	.000	-.000	-.579	R	I
33.	SALT	.001	-.002	-.171	R	-1.000
34.	PEATMOSS	.000	-.000	-.461	.022	1.000
35.	CLAY AND OTHER	.001	-.003	-.568	R	I
36.	ABRASIVES	.001	-.004	-.404	R	-1.000
37.	NON-METALLIC MINERALS	.007	-.012	-.197	613.705	-.999
38.	SAND AND GRAVELS	.001	-.005	-.456	R	-1.000
39.	STONE	.002	-.006	-.353	R	-1.000

I RESOURCE EXPORTS AND IMPORTS EQUAL ZERO.

R RESOURCE EXPORTS EQUAL ZERO.

TABLE A6

Direct and indirect trade with Japan in thirty-nine resources — average, 1967, 1968 and 1969

NO.	NAME OF CLASSIFICATION	PERCENTAGE OF RESOURCE EXPORTS (1)	TOTAL INDIRECT RESOURCE IMPORTS (2)	INDEX OF TRADE THROUGH COMMODITIES (3)	RATIO: INDIRECT SHIPMENTS TO DIRECT SHIPMENTS (4)	INDEX OF RESOURCE TRADE (5)
1.	LIVE ANIMALS	.045	-.054	.234	5.601	.916
3.	WHEAT	.014	-.067	.610	.018	1.000
4.	OTHER GRAIN	.011	-.009	.416	.088	.999
5.	MILK	.006	-.009	.142	R	I
6.	EGGS	.001	-.002	-.236	R	I
7.	HONEY AND BEESWAX	.000	-.000	-.556	.133	1.000
8.	NUTS, FRUITS, BERRIES	.001	-.064	-.317	R	-1.000
9.	VEGETABLES	.002	-.008	-.238	148.517	1.000
10.	HAY, GRASS AND NURSERY	.001	-.002	.184	.600	.227
11.	OIL SEED OIL NUTS	.002	-.011	-.415	.006	1.000
12.	HOPS	.000	-.000	.092	R	I
13.	TOBACCO	.000	-.000	.292	R	I
14.	FUR	.000	-.019	-.966	.060	.770
15.	WOOL IN THE GREASE	.001	-.021	-.869	R	I
16.	LOGS AND BOLTS	.153	-.106	.475	1.675	1.000
17.	POLES AND PIT PROPS	.001	-.003	-.293	.101	1.000
18.	PULPWOOD	.132	-.039	.740	266.868	1.000
19.	OTHER CRUDE WOOD	.000	-.001	-.011	R	-1.000
20.	CUSTOM FORESTRY	.034	-.018	.573	R	I
21.	FISH LANDINGS	.015	-.064	-.364	2.394	-.422
22.	METAL ORES	.412	-.235	.548	.309	.999

TABLE A6 continued

NO.	NAME OF CLASSIFICATION	PERCENTAGE OF TOTAL INDIRECT RESOURCE EXPORTS (1)	INDIRECT RESOURCE IMPORTS (2)	INDEX OF TRADE THROUGH COMMODITIES (3)	RATIO: INDIRECT SHIPMENTS TO DIRECT SHIPMENTS (4)	INDEX OF RESOURCE TRADE (5)
23.	RADIO-ACTIVE ORES	.047	-.026	.559	4.052	1.000
24.	IRON ORES	.011	-.098	-.639	.076	1.000
25.	GOLD AND PLATINUM ORES	.001	-.026	-.920	1.309	1.000
26.	COAL	.026	-.086	-.258	.241	1.000
27.	CRUDE MINERAL OILS	.059	-.092	.116	R	I
28.	NATURAL GAS	.002	-.005	-.122	R	I
29.	OTHER BITUMINOUS	.000	-.000	-.057	R	I
30.	SULPHUR	.004	-.004	.372	R	I
31.	ASBESTOS	.000	-.005	-.689	.004	1.000
32.	GYPSUM	.000	-.000	-.755	R	I
33.	SALT	.001	-.002	.098	R	I
34.	PEATMOSS	.000	-.000	.081	R	I
35.	CLAY AND OTHER	.001	-.005	-.321	R	I
36.	ABRASIVES	.001	-.003	-.126	R	I
37.	NON-METALLIC MINERALS	.009	-.015	.108	11.757	1.000
38.	SAND AND GRAVELS	.001	-.010	-.576	R	I
39.	STONE	.003	-.011	-.309	43.685	1.000

[I] RESOURCE EXPORTS AND IMPORTS EQUAL ZERO.

[R] RESOURCE EXPORTS EQUAL ZERO.

TABLE A7

Direct and indirect trade with UK, in thirty-nine resources – average 1967, 1968 and 1969

NO. NAME OF CLASSIFICATION	PERCENTAGE OF TOTAL INDIRECT RESOURCE EXPORTS (1)	INDIRECT RESOURCE IMPORTS (2)	INDEX OF TRADE THROUGH COMMODITIES (3)	RATIO: INDIRECT SHIPMENTS TO DIRECT SHIPMENTS (4)	INDEX OF RESOURCE TRADE (5)
1. LIVE ANIMALS	.030	-.087	.137	66.810	-.083
3. WHEAT	.012	-.021	.373	.045	1.000
4. OTHER GRAIN	.011	-.031	.154	.481	1.000
5. MILK	.021	-.015	.691	R	I
6. EGGS	.001	-.003	.039	R	-1.000
7. HONEY AND BEESWAX	.000	-.000	.252	.091	.964
8. NUTS, FRUITS, BERRIES	.004	-.011	.167	.464	1.000
9. VEGETABLES	.007	-.018	.230	3.136	.980
10. HAY, GRASS AND NURSERY	.001	-.002	.389	.423	.594
11. OIL SEED OIL NUTS	.009	-.025	.167	.267	.997
12. HOPS	.000	-.002	-.935	.095	.774
13. TOBACCO	.055	-.004	.964	R	I
14. FUR	.000	-.010	-.670	.025	.479
15. WOOL IN THE GREASE	.061	-.032	-.866	3.772	-.372
16. LOGS AND BOLTS	.091	-.024	.871	93.137	.998
17. POLES AND PIT PROPS	.001	-.002	.213	290.388	1.000
18. PULPWOOD	.073	-.048	.707	15.693	1.000
19. OTHER CRUDE WOOD	.001	-.061	.321	R	I
20. CUSTOM FORESTRY	.020	-.009	.781	R	I
21. FISH LANDINGS	.037	-.006	.913	2.576	.881
22. METAL ORES	.480	-.251	.763	7.817	.873

TABLE A7 continued

NO. NAME OF CLASSIFICATION	PERCENTAGE OF RESOURCE EXPORTS (1)	TOTAL INDIRECT RESOURCE IMPORTS (2)	INDEX OF TRADE THROUGH COMMODITIES (3)	RATIO: INDIRECT SHIPMENTS TO DIRECT SHIPMENTS (4)	INDEX OF RESOURCE TRADE (5)
23. RADIO-ACTIVE ORES	.055	-.028	.768	.945	1.000
24. IRON ORES	.010	-.078	-.345	.141	1.000
25. GOLD AND PLATINUM ORES	.001	-.022	-.708	.011	1.000
26. COAL	.023	-.079	.065	R	I
27. CRUDE MINERAL OILS	.037	-.119	.092	R	I
28. NATURAL GAS	.002	-.005	.096	R	I
29. OTHER BITUMINOUS	.000	-.000	.148	R	-1.000
30. SULPHUR	.003	-.064	.464	1.964	1.000
31. ASBESTOS	.001	-.009	-.603	.013	.996
32. GYPSUM	.000	-.001	-.610	R	-1.000
33. SALT	.001	-.003	.346	306.408	-.920
34. PEATMOSS	.000	-.000	.372	R	I
35. CLAY AND OTHER	.001	-.005	-.151	281.135	-.998
36. ABRASIVES	.001	-.005	-.080	R	-1.000
37. NON-METALLIC MINERALS	.007	-.017	.203	1.052	.600
38. SAND AND GRAVELS	.001	-.009	-.212	R	-1.000
39. STONE	.003	-.011	-.049	408.627	-.720

I RESOURCE EXPORTS AND IMPORTS EQUAL ZERO.

R RESOURCE EXPORTS EQUAL ZERO.

Bibliography

Baldwin, Robert E. (1971) 'Determinants of the commodity structure of US trade.' *American Economic Review* 61, 126-62

Ball, D.S. (1970) 'Factor intensity reversals in international comparisons of factor costs and factor use.' *Journal of Political Economy* 74, 77-80

Bardhan, V. Pranab (1965) 'International differences in production functions, trade and factor prices.' *Economic Journal* 75, 81-7

Bertrand, Trent J. (1972) 'An extension of the n-factor case of factor proportions theory.' *Kyklos* 25, 592-6

Bhagwati, Jagdish (1972) 'The Heckscher-Ohlin theorem in the multi-commodity case.' *Journal of Political Economy* 80, 1052-5

Christ, Carl F. (1960) *Econometric Models and Methods* (New York: John Wiley & Sons)

Eastman, H.C. and S. Stykolt (1967) *The Tariff and Competition in Canada* (Toronto: Macmillan)

Economic Council of Canada (1975) *Looking Outward* (Ottawa)

Ellis, Howard S. and Lloyd A. Metzler, eds, (1950) *Readings in the Theory of International Trade* (Philadelphia: Blakiston)

Grey, Rodney de C. (1973) *The Development of the Canadian Anti-Dumping System* (Montreal: The Private Planning Association)

Harkness, Jon and John F. Kyle (1975) 'Factors influencing United States comparative advantage.' *Journal of International Economics* 5, 153-65

Heckscher, Eli F. (1919) 'The effect of foreign trade on the distribution of income.' *Ekonomik Tidskrift* 21, 497-512

Hufbauer, G.C. (1970) 'The impact of national characteristics and technology on the commodity composition of trade in manufactured goods.' In Raymond Vernon, ed., *The Technology Factor in International Trade* (New York: Columbia University Press)

Jones, R.W. (1956-7) 'Factor proportions and the Heckscher-Ohlin theorem.' *Review of Economic Studies* 24, 1-10

Leontief, Wassily (1954) 'Domestic production and foreign trade; the American capital position re-examined.' *Economica Internazionale* 7, 9-45

Leontief, Wassily (1956) 'Factor proportions and the structure of American trade: further theoretical and empirical analysis.' *Review of Economics and Statistics* 38, 386-407

Leontief, Wassily (1964) 'International factor costs and factor use.' *American Economic Review* 54, 335-45

Melvin, James R. (1969) 'Increasing returns to scale as a determinant of trade.' *Canadian Journal of Economics* 2, 389-402

Michaely, Michael (1964) 'Factor proportions in international trade: current state of the theory.' *Kyklos* 17, 529-50

Minhas, Bagicha Singh (1963) *An International Comparison of Factor Cost and Factor Use* (Amsterdam: North Holland Publishing)

Ohlin, Bertil (1933, rev. 1967) *Interregional and International Trade* (Cambridge, Mass.: Harvard University Press)

Philpot, Gordon (1970) 'Labour quality, returns to scale and elasticity of factor substitution.' *Review of Economic Statistics* 52, 194-9

Postner, Harry H. assisted by Don Gilfix (1975) *Factor Content of Canadian Trade: an input-output analysis* (Ottawa: Economic Council of Canada)

Report of the Federal Task Force on Agriculture (1969) *Canadian Agriculture in the Seventies*

Robinson, Joan (1941) 'Rising supply price.' *Economica* n.s. 8, 1-8

Robinson, Romney (1956) 'Factor proportions and comparative advantage.' *Quarterly Journal of Economics* 70, 169-92

Rybczynski, T.M. (1955) 'Factor endowment and relative commodity prices' *Economica* n.s. (November) 336-41

Samuelson, Paul A. (1953-4) 'Prices of factors and goods in general equilibrium.' *Review of Economic Studies* 21, 1-20

Statistics Canada (15-50, 1969) *The Input-Output Structure of the Canadian Economy* 1, 193

Stegeman, Klaus (1973) *Canadian Non-Tariff Barriers to Trade* (Montreal: Private Planning Association)

Stolper, Wolfgang F. and Paul A. Samuelson (1941-2) 'Protection and real wages.' *Review of Economic Studies* 9, 58-73

Travis, William P. (1964) *The Theory of Trade and Protection* (Cambridge, Mass.: Harvard University Press)

Travis, William P. (1972) 'Production, trade, and protection when there are many commodities and two factors.' *American Economic Review* 62, 87-106

Vanek, Jaroslav (1963) *The Natural Resource Content of United States Foreign Trade, 1870-1955* (Cambridge, Mass.: MIT Press)

Vanek, Jaroslav (1968) 'The Factor Proportions Theory: the n-factor case.' *Kyklos* 21, 749-56

Weiser, Lawrence A. (1968) 'Changing factor requirements of United States foreign trade.' *Review of Economics and Statistics* 50, 356-60

Williams, James R. (1970) 'The resource content of international trade.' *Canadian Journal of Economics* 3, 121

Williams, James R. (forthcoming) *The Canadian Tariff and Canadian Industry: A Multisectoral Analysis* (Toronto: University of Toronto Press)

Wonnacott, Ronald J. and Paul Wonnacott (1967) *Free Trade Between the United States and Canada: The Potential Economic Effects* (Cambridge, Mass.: Harvard University Press)

Yahr, Merle I. (1968) 'Human capital and factor substitution in the CES production function.' In Peter B. Kenen and Roger Lawrence, eds. *The Open Economy: Essays on International Trade and Finance* (New York: Columbia University Press)